Basic Training

Les Christie

Paul Woods

David C. Cook Publishing Co.
Elgin, Illinois—Weston, Ontario

Custom Curriculum
Basic Training

© 1993 David C. Cook Publishing Co.

Published by David C. Cook Publishing Co.
850 North Grove Ave., Elgin, IL 60120
Cable address: DCCOOK
Series creator: John Duckworth
Series editor: Randy Southern
Editor: Randy Southern
Option writers: Eric Potter, Nelson E. Copeland, Jr., and Ellen Larson
Designer: Bill Paetzold
Cover illustrator: Arnie Ten
Inside illustrator: John Hayes
Printed in U.S.A.

ISBN: 0-7814-5002-0

CONTENTS

Sessions by Paul Woods
Options by Eric Potter, Nelson E. Copeland, Jr., and Ellen Larson

About the Authors

Paul Woods is an editor at Zondervan Publishing House and a past managing editor of Group Books. A former youth pastor, he helped create the *Pacesetter* series of youth resources for David C. Cook.

Eric Potter is a free-lance writer living in Fredericksburg, Virginia. He is a former editor for the David C. Cook Publishing Co. He has written for several David C. Cook series including *Hot Topics Youth Electives* and *Pathfinder Electives*.

Nelson E. Copeland, Jr. is a nationally known speaker and the author of several youth resources including *Great Games for City Kids* (Youth Specialties) and *A New Agenda for Urban Youth* (Winston-Derek). He is president of the Christian Education Coalition for African-American Leadership (CECAAL), an organization dedicated to reinforcing educational and cultural excellence among urban teenagers. He also serves as youth pastor at the First Baptist Church in Morton, Pennsylvania.

Ellen Larson is an educator and writer with degrees in education and theology. She has served as minister of Christian education in several churches, teaching teens and children, as well as their teachers. Her experience also includes teaching in public schools. She is the author of several books for Christian education teachers, and frequently leads training seminars for volunteer teachers. Ellen and her husband live in San Diego and are the parents of two daughters.

You've Made the Right Choice!

Thanks for choosing **Custom Curriculum**! We think your choice says at least three things about you:

(1) You know your group pretty well, and want your program to fit that group like a glove;

(2) You like having options instead of being boxed in by some far-off curriculum editor;

(3) You have a small mole on your left forearm, exactly two inches above the elbow.

OK, so we were wrong about the mole. But if you like having choices that help you tailor meetings to fit your kids, **Custom Curriculum** is the best place to be.

Going through Customs

In this (and every) **Custom Curriculum** volume, you'll find

• five great sessions you can use anytime, in any order.

• reproducible student handouts, at least one per session.

• a truckload of options for adapting the sessions to your group (more about that in a minute).

• a helpful get-you-ready article by a youth expert.

• clip art for making posters, fliers, and other kinds of publicity to get kids to your meetings.

Each **Custom Curriculum** session has three to five steps. No matter how many steps a session has, it's designed to achieve these goals:

• *Getting together.* Using an icebreaker activity, you'll help kids to be glad they came to the meeting.

• *Getting thirsty.* Why should kids care about your topic? Why should they care what the Bible has to say about it? You'll want to take a few minutes to earn their interest before you start pouring the "living water."

• *Getting the Word.* By exploring and discussing carefully selected passages, you'll find out what God has to say.

• *Getting the point.* Here's where you'll help kids make the leap from principles to nitty-gritty situations they are likely to face.

• *Getting personal.* What should each group member do as a result of this session? You'll help each person find a specific "next-step" response that works for him or her.

Each session is written to last 45 to 60 minutes. But what if you have less time—or more? No problem! **Custom Curriculum** is all about . . . options!

What Are My Options?

Every **Custom Curriculum** session gives you fourteen kinds of options:

• *Extra Action*—for groups that learn better when they're physically moving (instead of just reading, writing, and discussing).

• *Combined Junior High/High School*—to use when you're mixing age levels, and an activity or case study would be too "young" or "old" for part of the group.

• *Small Group*—for adapting activities that would be tough with groups of fewer than eight kids.

• *Large Group*—to alter steps for groups of more than twenty kids.

• *Urban*—for fitting sessions to urban facilities and multiethnic (especially African-American) concerns.

• *Heard It All Before*—for fresh approaches that get past the defenses of kids who are jaded by years in church.

• *Little Bible Background*—to use when most of your kids are strangers to the Bible, or haven't made a Christian commitment.

• *Mostly Guys*—to focus on guys' interests and to substitute activities they might be more enthused about.

• *Mostly Girls*—to address girls' concerns and to substitute activities they might prefer.

• *Extra Fun*—for longer, more "rowdy" youth meetings where the emphasis is on fun.

• *Short Meeting Time*—tips for condensing the session to 30 minutes or so.

• *Fellowship & Worship*—for building deeper relationships or enabling kids to praise God together.

• *Media*—to spice up meetings with video, music, or other popular media.

• *Sixth Grade*—appearing only in junior high/middle school volumes, this option helps you change steps that sixth graders might find hard to understand or relate to.

• *Extra Challenge*—appearing only in high school volumes, this option lets you crank up the voltage for kids who are ready for more Scripture or more demanding personal application.

Each kind of option is offered twice in each session. So in this book, you get *almost 150* ways to tweak the meetings to fit your group!

Customizing a Session

All right, you may be thinking. *With all of these options flying around, how do I put a session together? I don't have a lot of time, you know.*

We know! That's why we've made **Custom Curriculum** as easy to follow as possible. Let's take a look at how you might prepare an actual meeting. You can do that in four easy steps:

(1) *Read the basic session plan.* Start by choosing one or more of the goals listed at the beginning of the session. You have three to pick from: a goal that emphasizes *knowledge,* one that stresses *understanding,* and one that emphasizes *action.* Choose one or more, depending on what *you* want to accomplish. Then read the basic plan to see what will work for you and what might not.

(2) *Choose your options.* You don't *have* to use any options at all; the

basic session plan would work well for many groups, and you may want to stick with it if you have absolutely no time to consider options. But if you want a more perfect fit, check out your choices.

As you read the basic session plan, you'll see small symbols in the margin. Each symbol stands for a different kind of option. When you see a symbol, it means that kind of option is offered for that step. Turn to the page noted by the symbol and you'll see that option explained.

Let's say you have a small group, mostly guys who get bored if they don't keep moving. You'll want to keep an eye out for three kinds of options: Small Group, Mostly Guys, and Extra Action. As you read the basic session, you might spot symbols that tell you there are Small Group options for Step 1 and Step 3—maybe a different way to play a game so that you don't need big teams, and a way to cover several Bible passages when just a few kids are looking them up. Then you see symbols telling you that there are Mostly Guys options for Step 2 and Step 4—perhaps a substitute activity that doesn't require too much self-disclosure, and a case study guys will relate to. Finally you see symbols indicating Extra Action options for Step 2 and Step 3—maybe an active way to get kids' opinions instead of handing out a survey, and a way to act out some verses instead of just looking them up.

After reading the options, you might decide to use four of them. You base your choices on your personal tastes and the traits of your group that you think are most important right now. **Custom Curriculum** offers you more options than you'll need, so you can pick your current favorites and plug others into future meetings if you like.

(3) *Use the checklist.* Once you've picked your options, keep track of them with the simple checklist that appears at the end of each option section (just before the start of the next session plan). This little form gives you a place to write down the materials you'll need too—since they depend on the options you've chosen.

(4) *Get your stuff together.* Gather your materials; photocopy any Repro Resources (reproducible student sheets) you've decided to use. And . . . you're ready!

The Custom Curriculum Challenge

Your kids are fortunate to have you as their leader. You see them not as a bunch of generic teenagers, but as real, live, unique kids. You care whether you really connect with them. That's why you're willing to take a few extra minutes to tailor your meetings to fit.

It's a challenge to work with real, live kids, isn't it? We think you deserve a standing ovation for taking that challenge. And we pray that **Custom Curriculum** helps you shape sessions that shape lives for Jesus Christ and His kingdom.

—The Editors

Talking to Junior Highers about the "Basics"

by Les Christie

"Like arrows in the hands of a warrior are sons born in one's youth. Blessed is the man whose quiver is full of them" (Psalm 127:4, 5). Though directed primarily to parents, these verses also have something to say to junior high workers about the purpose of youth programs and activities. If children and youth are like arrows, then they must be aimed in a specific direction. If God has given us the task of caring for some of His "arrows," we must be sure we are guiding them toward the right target.

God has not left us wondering what that target might be. Colossians 1:28 states it clearly: "We proclaim him, admonishing and teaching everyone with all wisdom, so that we may present everyone perfect [mature, complete, whole] in Christ." The apostle Paul tells us we are also "to prepare God's people for works of service [ministry]" (Ephesians 4:12). Our job as youth workers is a sobering one. We are to bring young people to maturity in Christ and help prepare them for some form of ministry. We are to develop the leadership potential in youth. Our programs, Bible studies, and activities should be aimed at these objectives.

The topics "every Christian kid needs to know" addressed in this book will help you stay focused on these objectives. They are meaty issues. They are the building blocks of faith. If our junior highers don't know these things, what difference does all the other stuff in youth ministry make?

Know Who You're Talking To

Junior highers don't want to be treated like little children. They don't want to be talked down to. They are voicing their discontent and complaining that they want more. They want answers to their questions. They are at an age when they want to grow, not only physically but spiritually as well. Capitalize on this. By the time they reach high school, this desire can wane or flicker out. Fan the flame now.

Times have changed. Junior highers now face issues like alcohol and drug abuse, rock music, rebellion, dissatisfaction with the church, shop-lifting, and pornography. Things that in previous generations didn't hit until high school are now hitting junior highers squarely in the face. Junior highers want to know not only what to believe, but how to learn about God for themselves. The principles in this book are the foundation stones to build on.

Recognize Group Members' Limits

As you lead your junior highers through the session on "Words That Should Be Known," guard against using difficult terms to explain the issues being dealt with. Don't go over your group members' heads. Keep the words simple. Put the cookies on the lower shelf so that kids can reach them.

When you talk about God the Father, remember that some kids have terrible memories of their own fathers. One of our adult volunteers was a counselor at a junior high camp. A young man in his cabin said his only recollection of his father was from when the young man was just a few years old. He remembered being beaten by his father in a bathtub and seeing his own blood running down the drain. Telling a kid like this that he has a "heavenly Father" is not going to excite him. People don't like bad photos, images, or representations of themselves, and neither does God. Make sure the words you select accurately describe the God we love and serve.

In the session on "How to Talk to God," remember that prayer may be a strange, new concept to your kids. They may not have a clue what to include in a prayer. Don't have everyone hold hands in a circle and pray aloud. This can be extremely uncomfortable to a junior higher who has never prayed in public before. (Interestingly, many junior highers, when they do feel comfortable about praying out loud, are terrific. It's refreshing to listen to their candid, open prayers.)

Explore Ways to Motivate

It's been said that you can lead a horse to water, but you can't make it drink. However, you can encourage it to drink by giving it salt. By the same token, you can give a kid a Bible, but you can't make him or her read it. However, there are ways to *motivate* kids to read.

For a long time, I would tell young people how important it is to memorize Scripture, and they would nod sleepily and do nothing. It suddenly dawned on me that if I wanted them to memorize Scripture, *I* should memorize Scripture first! So I memorized Psalm 1 and recited it to my kids one Wednesday night at Bible study. I didn't say they should memorize it too. I merely mentioned how these verses had helped me the previous week.

The next Wednesday, four young people came to me before the meeting. "We've been memorizing some Bible verses," they said, "and we wondered if we could share them with you."

Those four kids shared in the Wednesday night youth meeting. The next week twenty students had memorized Scripture. What made the difference? I started practicing what I was preaching. Christ-centered youth workers can say with Paul, "Follow my example, as I follow the example of Christ" (I Corinthians 11:1).

Why did the disciples ask Jesus, "Lord, teach us to pray" (Luke 11:1)? Maybe it was because they had seen Jesus get up before dawn to pray, and they figured if prayer meant so much in His life, they needed it too! What are young people asking you to show them?

Provide Comfort and Assurance

In working through the "How to Fight Temptation" session, emphasize to your group members the importance of "putting Jesus first" in their lives. Point out that He will help them get through difficult times.

He will come alongside them during times of temptation. He will help them make it through.

At the 1992 Summer Olympics in Barcelona, Derek Redman was attempting to fulfill his lifelong dream of winning a gold medal in the 400-meter race. His goal was within sight as he came around the final turn. He could see the finish line. Then a pain shot up the back of his right thigh and he fell face first to the track. It was a hamstring pull. He would later tell *Sports Illustrated* that "it was with animal instinct that I pushed myself up and I began. Even though the race was over, I had to finish." The trainers were coming off both sides. The coaches were already emptying onto the track. He was pushing them away, hobbling and struggling toward the finish line. Then a big, burly man pushed through the crowd wearing a hat that said "Just Do It" and a T-shirt that said "Have you hugged your son today?" He went over to his son, took Derek's arm, and wrapped it around his shoulder. The reporters over-heard him say to his boy, "You don't have to do this." Derek said, "Dad, I started. I've got to finish." And the father said, "We began together and we will finish together." Derek did not walk away with the gold, but he walked away with an incredible memory of a father who would come out of the stands when he saw his son in pain and help him finish.

That's what Jesus does for us. When your teens put Jesus first, Jesus walks with them. They are not alone.

The last session of this book deals with "How to Be Christ's Body in the World." When your group members put Jesus first, He will help them reach out to a needy world—both in telling people about His love and in helping to meet the physical needs of hurting people.

What if Beethoven came up to you in the middle of writing his *Fifth Symphony* and asked you to finish it for him? Or what if Michelangelo requested you to finish chipping away at the slab of marble that would become the statue *David?* Or what if Leonardo da Vinci beckoned you to complete his half-finished painting of the *Mona Lisa?* I'd ask, "Where are the numbers?" Or, as one fellow said, "The only thing I can draw is flies." But what if Beethoven, da Vinci, or Michelangelo came into your body to assist you—so that it wasn't you writing, chipping, or painting, but the actual artist using *your* hands? Think of how you could impress your friends.

The material in this book will help your kids live out the Christian life, but they still need Jesus living the life through them. They can't do it on their own strength or power. Jesus infuses our lives as tea infuses hot water. Jesus uses our hands, legs, and minds as we release them to Him.

Les Christie is a twenty-six-year veteran of youth ministry. He has been at the same church for twenty-one years. Les is a sought-after, popular national convention speaker to both youth and adults. He has authored dozens of articles and books, including Unsung Heroes *(Youth Specialties). He is married, has two children, and lives in Placentia, California.*

The images on these two pages are designed to help you promote this course within your church and community. Feel free to photocopy anything here and adapt it to fit your publicity needs. The stuff on this page could be used as a flier that you send or hand out to kids—or as a bulletin insert. The stuff on the next page could be used to add visual interest to newsletters, calendars, bulletin boards, or other promotions. Be creative and have fun!

Do You
Know the Things
Every Christian
Needs to Know

?

If you want strong muscles, you've got to work out. The same is true if you want to be a strong Christian. We're going to start *Basic Training* and get our spiritual muscles in shape.

Who:

When:

Where:

Questions? Call:

Basic Training

Basic Training

Do you understand your Bible?

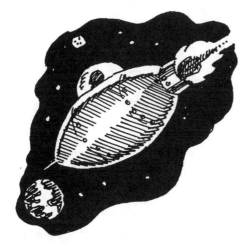

Coming soon to a planet near you.

You can beat temptation!
(I Corinthians 10:13)

Let's talk about it.

Words That Should Be Known

YOUR GOALS FOR THIS SESSION:

Choose one or more

☐ To help kids become familiar with key words and phrases of the Christian faith.

☐ To help kids understand that what we know about our faith can affect the way we live.

☐ To help kids commit to doing one thing to grow spiritually, based on the principles in this session.

☐ Other _____

Your Bible Base:

John 14:1-27
Ephesians 2:1-10; 4:1-16

STEP 1

Daffynitions

(Needed: Copies of Repro Resource 1, pencils, prizes)

OPTIONS

SMALL GROUP

LARGE GROUP

FELLOWSHIP & WORSHIP

EXTRA FUN

MEDIA

SHORT MEETING TIME

URBAN

JR. HIGH HIGH SCHOOL COMBINED

Distribute copies of "Daffynitions" (Repro Resource 1) and pencils. Explain that the object of this activity is to come up with definitions for the five words on the sheet. If group members don't know the real definitions of the words, they should make up logical-sounding or humorous definitions for them. Point out that the definitions at the bottom of the sheet may or may not be the correct definitions for some of the words.

Give group members a few minutes to work. Afterward, go through the words one at a time. Have each group member read his or her definition. Award prizes (perhaps bite-sized candy bars) to those who come up with the correct definitions. If no one comes up with the correct definition, vote as a group on who came up with the most logical-sounding and/or the most humorous guess, and award the person(s) a prize.

The correct definitions are as follows:

purser—an official on a passenger ship responsible for the tickets and accounts, as well as the comfort and welfare, of the passengers.

furze—a spiny, yellow-flowered, European evergreen shrub.

springe—a noose used to catch animals.

tuber—a thick, fleshy, round part of a plant root.

yaw—to deviate momentarily from the right course, as by a ship or an airplane.

After all the words have been discussed, ask: **If you'd lived your entire life without knowing the meaning of these five words, how do you think it might have affected you?** (Probably it wouldn't have made much of a difference.)

What if you'd never learned what junk food was? Or television? Or laughter? Or friends? How would your life be different? Get a few responses.

How do we decide which words and concepts are important to us and which aren't? (Words and concepts that affect our everyday lives or that are connected to our personal interests are important to us.)

Keys to Understanding

Say: **Let's say someone in this group has no idea what base-ball is. What key words and concepts would we need to explain to that person to help him or her get a basic understanding of baseball?** (Baseball, bat, bases, pitch, hit, catch, out, safe, runs, etc.)

Explain: **For every subject we choose to talk about, there are a few key words that we need to understand to help us grasp the subject. I'm going to call out a few subjects, and you call out key words for that subject.**

Call out the following words one at a time, and wait for group members to come up with at least five or six key words for each one. Some samples are given in case group members have trouble getting started.

- **Basketball** (Basketball, court, dribble, shoot, basket, foul, etc.)
- **Hair care** (Comb, brush, gel, shampoo, conditioner, perm, etc.)
- **Newspaper** (Reporters, headlines, articles, classifieds, comics, editorials, etc.)
- **Computer** (Keyboard, monitor, floppy disk, hard drive, memory, mouse, etc.)
- **Cooking** (Ingredients, pan, oven, mix, measuring devices, bake, etc.)
- **Car** (Engine, tires, steering wheel, gas, oil, driving, etc.)
- **History** (Exploration, war, revolution, treaty, king, dates, etc.)
- **Christian faith** (God, Jesus Christ, Holy Spirit, faith, sin, salvation, spiritual growth.)

Pay particular attention to group members' responses for the last subject. If group members don't mention all of the words in parentheses, mention them yourself.

Then say: **Our goal in this session is to get a better idea of what Christian faith is. To do that, we're going to explore some of the key words and concepts you just named.**

Wonderful Words

(Needed: Bibles, paper, chalkboard and chalk or newsprint and marker)

Write the following words on the board: *God, Jesus Christ, Holy Spirit, faith, sin, salvation,* and *spiritual growth.* Make sure you leave plenty of space between words to write down additional information.

Have group members form pairs. Assign each pair one of the following passages of Scripture: John 14:1-27; Ephesians 2:1-10; and Ephesians 4:1-16.

Distribute paper and pencils to each pair. Instruct the pairs to look up their assigned passages and write down as many statements as they can find concerning the words listed on the board. For instance, in John 14:1 Jesus says, "Trust in God; trust also in me." So group members might write down under "Jesus": "He wants us to trust in Him."

Explain that a couple of the categories, particularly "faith" and "spiritual growth," may take some extra thought. You may also want to point out that the Holy Spirit is often referred to as the "Comforter."

Give the pairs several minutes to work. When they're finished, go over the words one at a time. Ask each pair to share one statement it found concerning that word. Pairs will then continue alternating until all of the statements have been shared. Then do the same for the next word. As the pairs share their statements, write a word or two representing each statement on the board next to the word being described.

Use the following information to supplement the pairs' responses.

God
- Jesus wants us to trust in God (John 14:1).
- There is no way for us to get to God, except through Jesus (14:6).
- If we really know Jesus, we know God (14:7).
- If we love Jesus, we will be loved by God (14:21).
- God is loving and merciful (Ephesians 2:4).
- God gives us the gift of salvation (2:8).
- God expressed His kindness to us through Jesus (2:7).
- We are God's workmanship (2:10).
- There is one God and Father of all (4:6).

Jesus Christ
- Jesus wants us to believe in Him (John 14:1).
- Jesus is in heaven preparing a place for His people (14:2).
- Jesus is the only way for us to get to God (14:6).
- Jesus will do whatever believers ask in His name (14:13).

- Jesus gives us peace (14:27).
- Jesus gives gifts and talents to believers (Ephesians 4:11).
- Christ is the head of those who believe in Him (4:15).

Holy Spirit

- The Holy Spirit will be with us forever (John 14:16).
- The world cannot see the Holy Spirit (14:17).
- The Holy Spirit lives in us (14:17).
- The Holy Spirit teaches us and reminds us of the things Jesus said (14:26).
- The Holy Spirit unites believers (Ephesians 4:3).

Faith

- Faith involves believing that Jesus will come back for us (John 14:3).
- Faith involves believing that Jesus is the only way to God (14:6).
- Faith involves believing that Jesus is "in the Father, and that the Father is in [Him]" (14:10).
- Faith involves doing what Jesus has done (14:12).
- Faith involves believing that Jesus will do anything we ask in His name (14:13).
- Faith involves believing that the Holy Spirit is in us (14:17).
- Our faith in God's grace—and not our works—saves us (Ephesians 2:8, 9).

Sin

- Before a person becomes a Christian, he or she is "dead" in his or her sin (Ephesians 2:1).
- Before a person becomes a Christian, he or she lives to satisfy the cravings of his or her sinful nature (2:3).

Salvation

- Jesus is the only means of salvation, the only way to God (John 14:6).
- Salvation is the result of God's great love for us (Ephesians 2:4).
- We are saved only by God's grace, not by anything we do (2:8, 9).

Spiritual Growth

- Spiritual growth involves praying with the confidence that Jesus will do whatever we ask in His name (John 14:13).
- Spiritual growth involves obeying Jesus' commands (14:15).
- Spiritual growth involves being taught by the Spririt and reminded of Jesus' teachings (14:26).
- Spiritual growth involves being humble, gentle, patient, and willing to bear with others in love (Ephesians 4:1).
- Spiritual growth involves building up the body of Christ (4:12).
- Spiritual growth involves not allowing ourselves to be swayed by deceitful teaching (4:14).
- Spiritual growth involves speaking the truth in love to others (4:15).

Refer to the words listed on the board. Then ask: **How might having a better understanding of these words help us have a better understanding of the Christian faith?** (Understanding the basics gives us something to build on. When we're able to put things in perspective, we can better understand more complicated teachings.)

STEP 4

And the Words Became Flesh

(Needed: Bibles)

Have group members form teams of three or four. Assign each team one or more (depending on the size of your group) of the words on the board. Instruct each team to put together a 30-second skit demonstrating how a new understanding of the assigned word(s) could be put into action in a person's life. For example, a team that was assigned the "Holy Spirit" might create a skit in which the Holy Spirit reminds a person in trouble about a helpful passage from Scripture.

Give the teams a few minutes to prepare. Encourage them to look back at the Scripture passages for ideas. When they're finished, have them present their skits one at a time. After each skit, ask volunteers to suggest additional ways in which group members could put to work in their lives the things they've learned in Scripture.

Then ask: **How can the things we've learned in this session about our faith make a difference in the way we live out our Christianity?** (Some of the things give us new hope for the future and confidence that God loves us. Other things cause us to be grateful for what God has done for us.)

STEP 5

Circle of Thanks

Have group members stand and form a circle. Then say something like this: **God has revealed Himself and His plan for His people through the Bible. We've learned a bit more about that plan**

today. We can be thankful for what God has revealed to us about each of the words we've studied today. For our closing prayer, I'll say one of those words, and you call out things about that word that we can be thankful for.

Begin with "God" and then move through the list: Jesus Christ, Holy Spirit, faith, sin, salvation, and spiritual growth. Pause after each one for at least two or three statements of thankfulness. (However, "sin" might bring only one response: thankfulness that it can be forgiven.)

After going through all of the words, say: **Being thankful for these things is a start. Now let's commit ourselves to letting them make a difference in our lives. Close your eyes and think of one area of your life in which you might want to make a change, based on what you learned today. If you're willing to commit yourself to making that change, tell God about it silently. Then, if you want to, tell the group about it too.**

Give group members a moment of silence. Don't attempt to force group members to share if they don't want to. Encourage them to make the commitment to God even if they don't want to mention it aloud. If group members begin sharing their commitments, let it continue until there's a 10-second pause. Then wrap up the session by praying aloud.

DAF·*fy*·ni·tions

Your assignment is to come up with a definition for each of the five words below. If you don't know the actual definition of a word, make up one that sounds logical. Or make up one that's humorous. Either way, try to be as creative as possible in faking a definition.

To make things a little more confusing, we've included some defintions at the bottom of the page that may or may not go with some of the words. You decide.

PURSER—

furze—

springe—

tuber—

yaw—

One who carries money or other valuables for another person—often used by the wealthy in lieu of a pocketbook or wallet.

A spiny, yellow-flowered, European evergreen shrub.

An informal greeting, usually used to indicate agreement.

THE SEASON BETWEEN WINTER AND SUMMER (OLD ENGLISH SPELLING).

One who, while positioned in a rubber inner tube, allows himself to be propelled across the surface of a body of water by attaching the tube to a powerboat.

EXTRA ACTION

Step 2

Liven up the discussion of key words by playing charades. Have group members form teams. Assign one of the following categories—basketball, hair care, newspaper, computer, cooking, car, and history—to each team. Have each team brainstorm a list of key terms for its category without letting the other teams know. Then have the members of each team act out the key words, while other teams try to guess them. After all the teams have had a turn, bring up the category of "Christian Faith." Instruct your entire group to come up with a list of key terms for this category.

Step 3

Have group members play a game of "Not-So-Trivial Pursuit." Write the seven key terms—*God, Jesus Christ, Holy Spirit, faith, sin, salvation,* and *spiritual growth*—on the board. Have group members form pairs. Distribute several index cards and pencils to each pair. Assign one of the passages listed in the session to each pair. Instruct each pair to read its passage and come up with one question and answer (including the Scripture reference) for as many of the key terms as possible. (For example: "Who will be with us forever?" "The Holy Spirit" [John 14:16].) The pairs should write their questions and answers on their cards. (For the sake of reference, the pairs should also write down the appropriate key term on each card.) Collect the cards and sort them into piles, according to the key terms. Then have the pairs join together to form two teams. Choose a pile and begin the game with a question from it. If the player answers the question correctly, move to the next pile and have the next player on that team answer it. If a player answers incorrectly, move to the next pile and have a player from the other team answer the question. Continue moving through the piles in the same order until all of the questions have been asked. Keep a tally of correct answers, and award prizes to the winning team.

SMALL GROUP

Step 1

If your group is small and your kids know each other pretty well, you might want to try the following "guess-the-identity" activity to introduce the idea of key terms. Distribute index cards. Instruct each group member to write down three words or phrases that best sum up his or her identity. These key words and phrases may describe physical characteristics (blond, tall, muscular, etc.), interests (poet, cat lover, soccer star), or anything else involving the person's identity. Encourage group members to put some thought into their responses. Emphasize that you're looking for *the* three key words or phrases that best sum them up. When everyone is finished, collect and shuffle the cards. Then read each one aloud and have group members try to guess whose it is. Afterward, ask: **What are some key terms of "the Christian faith"?** (God, Jesus Christ, Holy Spirit, faith, sin, salvation, spiritual growth.)

Step 4

The skits may not work well since you may have as many people performing as watching. Instead distribute paper and markers and have group members (or pairs) draw cartoons or comic strips. The cartoons should depict situations in which people put into action their understanding of the key concepts of the Christian faith. For example, for the term "Holy Spirit," someone might draw a person in trouble who suddenly hears a disembodied voice reminding him or her of a Scripture verse.

LARGE GROUP

Step 1

Have group members form two teams. Give each team a dictionary. Instruct the members of each team to choose five words that they think the other team won't know. Team members should write down four definitions for each word—one of them real, and the other three fake. (After teams choose their words, they may want to assign pairs or trios to write the definitions.) When everyone is finished, have one team read aloud one of its words and the four accompanying definitions. The other team will then try to guess which is the correct definition. Have the teams alternate reading their words until all of the words have been read. Award prizes to the team that gets the most correct answers.

Step 3

In a large group, the Bible study may take a long time if you have to wait for pairs to search for all seven key terms in their assigned passage. To save time, you might want to assign passages another way. Have group members form three teams. Assign one of the Scripture passages to each team. Assuming that each team has at least seven members, have the teams assign each member one of the key terms listed on the board. Each team member will then search the team's passage for statements that have to do with his or her assigned term. When the teams report back to the rest of the group, each member will briefly share his or her findings.

Step 4

Help your group members apply the key-word concepts to real-life situations. Have your group members brainstorm a list of the top five or ten problems that kids their age face. Write these problems on the board as they are named. If the kids have trouble coming up with a list, encourage them to think of situations or problems associated with school, church, youth group, family, dating, sports, etc. After you've completed the list, have group members form teams of two or three. Instruct each team to choose a problem from the list and then come up with a skit showing how an understanding of one of the key terms (from Step 3) might help someone facing that problem. (For example, let's say one of the problems on the board is "being tempted to drink/take drugs." A team might come up with a skit in which someone who is tempted to drink keeps being reminded by the voice of the Holy Spirit of relevant Bible verses.)

Step 5

Since kids who've "heard it all before" will probably have a good handle on the knowledge and understanding of the objectives of this session, emphasize the commitment aspect. Before you do the circle of thanks, distribute pencils and slips of paper. Have group members write "Because …" near the top of the paper and "I will" near the bottom. Then instruct the kids to choose one of the key-word principles and think of a way it could change their actions. (They could use the skits or list you developed in Step 4.) Have them write the statement of biblical truth next to "Because …" and the commitment they will make after "I will." For example: "Because spiritual growth involves being humble, gentle, and patient, I will quit yelling at my brothers and sisters for hogging the bathroom."

Step 2

In this first session of the series, it might be helpful to get an idea of what your group members know about the Christian faith. Go through the first seven items in the "key words" activity. Then ask: **When you hear people talking about being a Christian or going to church, what are some of the words and phrases they use?** List the words and phrases on the board as they are named. If you have time, ask volunteers to share what they think each word or phrase means. As necessary, introduce some of the other key terms of the Christian faith that weren't named by group members.

Step 3

You may need to help your group members locate the Books of John and Ephesians in their Bibles. You may also need to introduce the passages with some background information. Explain that John is one of the Gospels, that it tells about Jesus' life on earth. Chapter 14 is Jesus' last night with His disciples. He knows He's been betrayed, that He'll be crucified, and that after the Resurrection He'll go to be with God. He's trying to prepare His disciples for these coming events, to give His final words of wisdom to them. Ephesians is one of the letters that the apostle Paul wrote to churches. In the first half of the book, he stresses the riches that Christians have in Christ (such as God's mercy and grace); in the second half, he gives practical advice about using those riches to live lives that please God.

Step 1

Use the following game to introduce the idea of key words and to help group members get to know each other better. Distribute index cards and pencils. Instruct group members to think of a hobby or interest that is important to them, that contributes to who they are. Have them pick three words that have something to do with that hobby or interest and write the words on their cards. Encourage them to choose words that aren't very obvious. For example, if the hobby is photography, instead of writing "camera" or "film," the person could write "developer" or "enlarger." One at a time, have each person read his or her words. Then have the rest of the group try to guess the person's hobby or interest. Afterward, point out that each set of words may be important to the person who read the words, but may not be important to others. Another way to do this activity is to have kids write their words on a card, tape the card to their back, and then mill around reading each other's cards and trying to guess as many people's hobbies as possible.

Step 5

Have group members form seven teams. (If you have a small group, "teams" may consist of only one or two people.) Assign each team one of the seven key terms (from Step 3). Have each team write a short prayer based on its term, expressing thanks for the truths revealed in that term. Then choose one or two hymns or songs whose lyrics are relevant to the topic. ("Wonderful Words of Life" could work.) Sing a verse of the song, have one or two teams read their prayers, sing another verse, and so on. Close with a final word of prayer. If you like, you could also have teams find Scripture verses relating to their terms, perhaps from the passages studied in Step 3. Then you could combine singing, praying, and Scripture reading.

Step 3

Instead of having group members work in pairs, have them form six teams. Assign each team one (or more) of the terms on the board. Instruct each team to read John 14:1-27; Ephesians 2:1-10; and Ephesians 4:1-16 and find at least four statements that have to do with its term(s). After a few minutes, have each team share its findings. (If possible, you may want to write the teams' responses on the board as they are named.)

Step 4

Don't limit the teams' method of expression to simply creating a skit. Instead, offer a wide variety of options for demonstrating how an understanding of one of the key terms could be put into action. Some teams may write a letter or song; others may design a puzzle or draw a comic strip; still others may use mime or interpretive dance. After teams have chosen their methods, give them several minutes to prepare their presentations. Then have each team present its work to the group.

Step 2

Have group members form two teams. Instruct each team to write down five or six sports or hobbies. Then, for each sport/ hobby, team members should come up with a list of five words that are associated with the sport. Encourage the teams to think of terms that most people probably wouldn't know. (For example, a team might choose "archery" as one of its sports. One of the words the team might use is "fletch," which means to put feathers on arrows.) Each team will then read the words one at a time while the other team tries to guess the sport/hobby associated with the words. The object of the game is to guess the sport/hobby using the least number of clues. After the game, discuss how each subject has key words important to it. Then ask kids to list key words related to the Christian faith.

Step 4

You will need a football and two round balls. Have group members start thinking about situations that they face as teenage guys. They might think of everyday situations or once-in-a-lifetime events, things that upset them or things that make them happy. Among the situations guys might think of are puberty, voice change, math class, first dates, etc. While group members are thinking, have them form a circle and begin passing the balls. The round balls must be passed around the circle from person to person, either to the right or left. The football can be passed the same way or across the circle. Explain that you won't watch them pass the balls, but when you shout **Freeze,** they have to stop; then whoever has the football has to call out a situation, which you will write on the board. Keep playing until you have a good list. Then discuss how an understanding of the key words of the Christian faith could be put into action in these situations.

Step 1

Before the session, come up with a list of unusual or uncommon words. For each word, make a pair of cards. Write the word on one card and its definition on the other. Make enough cards so that you'll have one for each group member. During the session, have each kid tape a card to his or her back. Then have group members mill around trying to find their partner (matching the word and definition). When they think they have a pair, they should come to you for final approval. (You may want to keep a master list of the words and definitions.) When all group members have found their partners, discuss what makes words important. If you have time, you could play "Daffynitions" too, and save the discussion for afterward.

Step 5

Reinforce this session's emphasis on key words by playing a word game. Have group members sit in a circle. Give them a ball to pass around the circle. Don't look at them as they pass the ball. Periodically stop the action and name a letter. Whoever has the ball at that point has to name three words that begin with that letter. If he or she can't do it in five seconds, he or she is out. As a variation of this game, name a sport, hobby, or profession when you stop the action, and have the person holding the ball name three terms associated with it. For example, if you said, "police work," the person might say "squad car," "gun," and "badge."

Step 1

Before the session, use the words on the "Daffynitions" sheet to make a multiple-choice vocabulary quiz. Tape-record this quiz so that you can play it for the kids during the session. For each word, say the word, then give four choices ("a" through "d"). If you want, include the real definition along with fake ones you make up. Let "d" stand for "None of the above." During the session, distribute paper and pencils. Play the tape and have kids take the quiz. Afterward, give the correct answers. Get a show of hands to see how many kids were fooled by the definitions. Then use the discussion questions in the session.

Step 2

Bring in a collection of specialty magazines devoted to a particular hobby, sport, or other interest. Distribute the magazines along with paper and pencils. (You may want kids to work in pairs or small groups.) As group members look through the magazines, have them make a list of key terms related to the magazine's specialty, along with definitions of those terms. After kids have shared and discussed the terms they discovered, have them come up with key terms for the Christian faith.

Step 1

Either skip this step or shorten it in the following way. Distribute the "Daffynitions" sheet, but don't have kids make up definitions. Instead, have them choose which of the definition(s) at the bottom of the sheet are real and which word(s) they go with. After group members have made their guesses, go over the sheet, seeing how many guessed correctly. Have volunteers take a guess or two at the real definitions of the words; then read the correct answers if they don't guess right.

Step 2

After introducing the basic idea with the baseball example, shorten the rest of the step by choosing only one or two terms from the list (perhaps basketball and hair care). After discussing these terms, spend some time talking about key terms of the Christian faith.

Step 1

Here are some other "daffynitions" you might use with an urban group.

Kuumba—a term meaning creativity, as expressed in the African-American holiday Kwanzaa.

Chumpie—a slang expression referring to an object or thing you know, but cannot identify.

Bezique—a card game, similar to pinochle, played with 64 cards.

Feria—an Hispanic market festival that usually observes a religious holiday.

Bibcock—a faucet with a bent-down nozzle.

Step 3

To the "wonderful words" list include *hope*. It is important that urban adolescents realize *hope* is a religious term that has its substance found in God. Use the Scripture references from the session with the following reflections:

• Our hope begins with trust in God (John 14:1).

• Hope allows us not to be troubled (John 14:1).

• The grace and love of salvation gives hope (Ephesians 2:4).

• We can have the hope of heaven (Ephesians 2:6).

• We are called to one hope (Ephesians 4:4).

Step 1

Have group members form teams according to the schools they attend. Distribute paper and pencils to each team. Instruct the teams to come up with a list of ten words that a kid would need to know to fit in and/or survive at their school. If the teams have trouble getting started, suggest that they think about things like the following: the principal's name (or nickname), names of teachers to take or avoid, nicknames for things like the cafeteria or P. E., inside jokes, school-based slang (nothing crude), and so on. When everyone is finished, have each team read its list while the other teams try to guess the meaning or significance of the terms. Afterward, discuss why the terms are important to them.

Step 3

As much as possible, try to pair up junior highers with high schoolers for the Bible study activity. Some of the terms on the board are not immediately obvious in the assigned passages. Junior highers may have trouble "reading between the lines" to figure out what the passages are saying about faith or spiritual growth. Therefore, in the pairs, instruct junior highers to look for statements that refer to God, Jesus Christ, and the Holy Spirit ("Comforter"). Instruct high schoolers to look for statements that refer to faith, sin, salvation, and spiritual growth.

Step 3

Rather than having your sixth graders work in pairs, have them form teams of three or four. Assign each team one or more of the following Scripture passages: John 14:1-7; John 14: 8-13; John 14:14-27; Ephesians 2:1-10; and Ephesians 4:1-16. Instruct the members of each team to look up their assigned passage(s) and write down at least three statements they find regarding any of the seven key terms written on the board.

Step 4

Have group members form teams. Assign each team one or more of the key terms you wrote on the board in Step 3. Rather than having teams come up with skits, instruct each team to explain its assigned term to the rest of the group as if the term were completely new. Each team should spell and pronounce its term, use it in a variety of ways to help convey its meaning, and then give the group an opportunity to ask questions if the meaning is not clear.

Date Used:

Approx.
Time
_____

Step 1: Daffynitions
o Small Group
o Large Group
o Fellowship & Worship
o Extra Fun
o Media
o Short Meeting Time
o Urban
o Combined Junior High/High School
Things needed:

Step 2: Keys to Understanding _____
o Extra Action
o Little Bible Background
o Mostly Guys
o Media
o Short Meeting Time
Things needed:

Step 3: Wonderful Words _____
o Extra Action
o Large Group
o Little Bible Background
o Mostly Girls
o Urban
o Combined Junior High/High School
o Sixth Grade
Things needed:

Step 4: And the Words Became Flesh _____
o Small Group
o Heard It All Before
o Mostly Girls
o Mostly Guys
o Sixth Grade
Things needed:

Step 5: Circle of Thanks _____
o Heard It All Before
o Fellowship & Worship
o Extra Fun
Things needed:

2 How to Talk to God

YOUR GOALS FOR THIS SESSION:

Choose one or more

☐ To help kids recognize that God wants us to communicate with Him through prayer.

☐ To help kids understand that prayer doesn't have to be something awkward and mysterious.

☐ To help kids increase the frequency of their communication with God through prayer.

☐ Other _____

Your Bible Base:

Matthew 6:5-15; 7:7-11
Philippians 4:6, 7

Guess What!

(Needed: Slips of paper prepared according to instructions, container, clock or watch with second hand, paper, scarf or string [optional], prize [optional])

Before the meeting, write the names of the following objects on separate slips of paper: a ball bearing, a two-by-four board, a cardboard box, a coatrack, a toy wagon, antifreeze, a CD player, computer paper, a water heater, and a walnut tree.

When group members arrive, explain: **We're going to begin this session by playing a description game. I'll give one of you a slip of paper with the name of an object on it. That person must then describe the object to the rest of the group without using any form of any words within the name of the object. For example, if the object were "saltshaker," you couldn't use "a container for something salty" or "something you shake a white substance out of." Also, you may not use any gestures in describing your objects. So to prevent this, you must keep your hands behind your back during your description.**

We'll time each person. The one who has his or her object guessed fastest will be the winner. But anyone who uses any form of a word in the name of the object will be automatically disqualified.

Choose a volunteer and let him or her draw a slip of paper. After the person reads the name of the object, take the slip back so that you know what the object is. To add a little more interest, use a scarf or string to tie the person's hands behind his or her back. Give the person a "go" signal, and keep track of the time. You'll be the judge of when the object is guessed correctly.

Give as many group members as possible a chance to describe an object. If you have more than ten kids in your group, you may want to come up with more objects to be guessed.

After the last person takes his or her turn, declare a winner. You might want to give the winner a prize.

Then ask: **What made it difficult to describe these objects?** (Responses might include the following: I couldn't use the words that would work best; I couldn't use my hands to make gestures; I was too nervous to think; etc.)

What helped the fastest people do so well? (They thought fast. They had easy objects. They knew just what to say.)

Say: **Communication was the key to this game. And communication is a key to many parts of our lives. Sometimes communication is easy; sometimes it's not. But it's always important.**

Adventurous Communicators

(Needed: Paper, pencils)

Let's do a quick exercise to show how important communication is.

Have group members form teams of three or four. Distribute paper and pencils to each team. Explain: **Imagine that you and your teammates are passengers on the Starship Galactica, and you're on a mission to explore new worlds in space. You've just discovered that your ship is about to come in contact with a remote planet. You've also discovered that the inhabitants of this planet are far more powerful and advanced than you are. In fact, they have the power to completely destroy your ship. The captain of the Starship has come to you and your teammates for help. He wants you to write a message for him to send to the leader of the alien race.**

Give the teams a few minutes to write their messages. When everyone is finished, have each team read its message to the rest of the group.

Afterward, ask: **What did you want to communicate in your message to the leader of the alien race?** (Some may have wanted to communicate respect and reverence. Others may have wanted to emphasize the peaceful nature of the Starship's mission.)

What circumstances made it difficult to come up with a message to send? (Some might mention that they couldn't see the person they were communicating with—they had no idea what the leader of the alien race was like. Others might mention that they didn't know whether or not their message was being heard or understood. Still others might mention that it was an emergency situation—one wrong word in the message might have offended the alien leader and provoked him to destroy the Starship.)

Do you see any similarities between approaching the alien

OPTIONS

EXTRA ACTION

HEARD IT ALL BEFORE

MOSTLY GUYS

SHORT MEETING TIME

JR. HIGH / HIGH SCHOOL COMBINED

leader with a message and approaching God in prayer? Group members may not make the connection at first. Encourage them to think about it for a moment. Some may point out that, like the alien leader, God is more powerful than we are. In fact, God has power over life and death. Others might mention that we can't see God when we pray, just as they couldn't see the alien leader they were communicating with. Still others might say that we have no absolute proof that God hears and responds to our prayers, just as they didn't know whether the alien leader heard or understood their messages.

How is approaching God in prayer different from approaching the alien leader? (Of course, God is more powerful and intelligent than any alien—He can understand any message we send to Him. We know that God cares about us. God wants us to pray to Him—He wants to hear from us. Because God is our heavenly Father, we don't have to worry about whether He will destroy us or not.)

Explain: **Our topic today is prayer—communication with God. Sometimes we take it for granted; other times we don't know quite what to say or do. In this session, we're going to work on understanding prayer a little better.**

STEP
3

Communication Clarified

(Needed: Copies of Repro Resource 2, pencils, Bibles)

Have group members form pairs. Explain: **When builders and construction companies begin a new project, they need specifications—guidelines that tell them exactly what they have to do. Let's think about our prayer lives as a "project" we're working on. Like the builders and construction companies, our first step should be to get some specifications— prayer guidelines that tell us what we need to do.**

Where do you think we might get these guidelines? (The Bible.)

Distribute copies of "Prayer Specifications" (Repro Resource 2) and pencils. Have partners work together to fill out the sheet. To save time, you may want to divide the questions among the pairs, so that each pair is working on different questions. Give the pairs several minutes to work. When they're finished, have them report their findings. Use the following information to supplement their responses.

Who should we pray to? (God, our Father in heaven.)

When should we pray? (Philippians 4:6 says we should pray about "everything." That would seem to indicate that we should be in contact with God regularly every day.)

Where should we pray? (In our rooms, in private.)

How should we pray? (Humbly; with forgiveness for those who have wronged us; persistently; with thanksgiving.)

How should we not pray? (As though we are trying to be seen and admired by other people for our prayers; with "babbling"; without forgiveness for those who have wronged us; anxiously.)

What should we ask for in prayer? (That God's will be done; our daily provisions; forgiveness for the things we've done wrong; deliverance from temptation and evil.)

What attitude should we have about prayer? (Humility; confidence that God knows our needs; patience; confidence that God will answer our prayers for our ultimate good.)

What kind of response to our prayers are we promised? (Reward for prayers done in secret; forgiveness as we forgive others; that which we ask for will be given to us; that which we seek, we will find; good gifts from God.)

What is the ultimate result of prayer? (The peace of God, which is beyond our ability to understand, will guard our hearts and minds.)

Ask: **How is communicating with God similar to communicating with people?** (Both involve talking and listening. Both can involve our requests for help. Both can involve our requests for forgiveness. Both can involve our thanksgiving.)

How is communicating with God different from communicating with people? (We sometimes close our eyes and bow our heads to talk with God. We can't see God when we talk to Him. God can give us anything He wants; people can't.)

Say: **In many ways, praying is similar to communicating with people. But there are some big differences, as we've just seen. God wants us to communicate with Him because He cares about us. And if we love God, we will want to communicate with Him like we communicate with people we care about.**

Hows and Whys

(Needed: Slips of paper, pencils)

Distribute slips of paper. Instruct group members to write down any questions they have about prayer. Emphasize that there is no such thing as a dumb question. If someone is uncertain about any aspect of prayer, he or she should write it down and not worry about whether the question is foolish or not. Group members should not write their names on the slips, so that the questions remain anonymous. After a minute or two, gather the slips and begin the following discussion.

Ask: **When we pray, are there special words we should use? Explain.** Group members may differ in opinion on this question. Some may say no, that we can talk to God just like we do our friends—using the same casual language and attitude. Others may say yes, that we need to be polite when we talk to God and that we should say "amen" when we're finished.)

Why do we usually close our eyes when we pray? (To help us shut out things that might distract us; to help us concentrate on communicating with God.)

How often should we pray? Pay attention to group members' opinions. Some may say we need to pray every day, all the time. Others may say we need to pray before every meal and before going to sleep. Still others may say that we need to pray only when we're in trouble.

How does God communicate with us? (Most of the time He communicates with us through the Bible. He also gives us a sense of peace when we choose to do things His way. He uses the Holy Spirit as a translator or "go-between" to help us understand things.)

How does God answer prayer? (He causes things to happen or prevents them from happening. He helps us find answers we ask for. He gives us a sense of peace when we're worried or scared.)

Does God always answer prayer? Explain. (Yes, He always answers prayer. Sometimes His answer is no. Sometimes He wants us to wait for His timing. Sometimes He gives us what we *need*, even if it's not what we asked for.)

At this point, refer to the questions about prayer your group members wrote down. As a group, discuss any of them you haven't addressed yet. Don't just answer the questions for your group members. Let them get involved in answering them. Suggest that they look at the Scripture passages listed on Repro Resource 2 for help.

STEP
5

We Have a Prayer

Summarize: **God wants us to communicate with Him because He cares about us. He wants us to share our daily concerns and joys with Him. He wants us to tell Him thanks for all He does for us. And He wants to give us exactly what we need. We don't have to pray in fancy words or long sentences. We can even pray just by directing our thoughts toward God.**

Think about how often you pray. Then think about how you might be able to help yourself pray a little more often. Maybe you can try to pray every morning or every night—or both. Choose something you think you can do and ask God to help you follow through on doing it.

Have group members stand in a circle. Say: **We're going to thank God for the opportunity to pray and that He cares enough about us to answer our prayers. We'll say together, "Thank you, God, for . . ." and then wait for someone to complete the sentence with a word or phrase related to prayer. Then we'll say, "Thank you, God, for . . ." again and someone else will respond. After a few prayers, I'll wrap up our prayer time.**

Don't be afraid to wait for the first couple of group members to respond. But don't let it drag on too long either. Unless group members seem unusually responsive, close your prayer time after five or six responses.

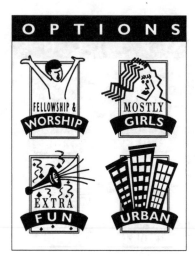

O P T I O N S

FELLOWSHIP &
WORSHIP

MOSTLY
GIRLS

EXTRA
FUN

URBAN

PRAYER
SPECIFICATIONS

Read Matthew 6:5-15; 7:7-11 and Philippians 4:6, 7. Then fill in the prayer information requested below.

Who should we pray to?

When should we pray?

Where should we pray?

How should we pray?

How should we not pray?

What should we ask for in prayer?

What attitude should we have about prayer?

What kind of response to our prayers are we promised?

What is the ultimate result of prayer?

Step 2

Bring several large and/or odd-shaped objects (an old tire, milk crates, a large sheet of plastic, etc.). Have your group members work together in creating the "world's most difficult obstacle course," using the objects you've brought in and any other objects they can find in the meeting area (tables, chairs, etc.). Give group members several minutes to complete the course. When they're finished, ask for volunteers to run the course. Award prizes to those who run the course in less than a minute (or 30 seconds, depending on the size of the course). Use the activity to lead into a discussion on the obstacles we face in trying to pray.

Step 3

Have group members form pairs. Distribute paper, pencils, and a copy of Repro Resource 2 to each pair. Instruct the pairs to read the assigned passages and, using the sheet as a guide, to make a true or false statement about prayer for use in a true-false quiz. On their papers the pairs should write the statement, the answer, and a Scripture reference that supports the answer. For example, a pair might write "We should pray at least six times a day." The answer is false. The pair might use Philippians 4:6 as its reference. The verse says to pray about "everything," but it doesn't specify a number of times. The pairs should also write a "penalty activity" for those who answer the question incorrectly during the quiz. The penalties should be humorous, but not humiliating. (For example, a penalty might involve reciting the words to "Yankee Doodle" while talking like Elmer Fudd.) When everyone is finished, collect the slips, read each statement aloud, and have kids give their answers. If they think a statement is true, they should stand up; if they think it's false, they should remain seated. After group members have responded, give the correct answer. Then have all who answered incorrectly perform the assigned "penalty activity."

Step 1

The opening activity is uncomplicated enough to work well with a large group. But if you have a small group, you might want to try an activity with a little more challenge and involvement. Try a game of art charades. Before the session, you'll need to prepare several cards, each with a common saying or proverb on it. (For example, you might use "A stitch in time saves nine" on one of the cards.) When the session begins, give each group member one card, which he or she may not show to anyone else. One at a time, have group members come to the board and "draw" their sayings or proverbs, using pictures instead of words. (For example, "stitch" might be represented by a picture of a sewing needle and thread going through a piece of cloth; "time" might be represented by a picture of a clock; "saves" might be represented by ... well, that's the tricky part.) Keep track of whose saying is guessed the fastest. After everyone has played, discuss why some sayings were easier to guess than others. (It may be due to the fact that some sayings are better known than others, that some sayings are easier to represent with pictures, or that the person drawing was a better artist than the others.)

Step 4

Have group members form teams. Give each team paper, pencils, and markers. Instruct each team to write and design a "product brochure," describing prayer as a product. Suggest that the teams might want to include the following kinds of information: a description of what the product is, details of some of its features and benefits, directions for how to use and how not to use it, and instructions for how to maintain it. After everyone is finished, have each team present and explain its brochures.

Step 1

Since a large group provides you with a good audience, modify the guessing game to make it like the old game show "Password." You will need ten pairs of contestants. One person in each pair will give clues; the other will guess. Assign each pair one of the words from the session (a ball bearing, a two-by-four board, a cardboard box, etc.). Send the guesser out of the room for a moment while you tell the rest of the group what the word is. Then bring the guesser back in and have his or her partner begin giving one-word clues, trying to get the guesser to guess the word. You may want to time the pairs or keep track of how many clues it takes to guess the word. Award prizes to the winning pair. Afterward, discuss the communication between partners. Ask: **What worked best and why? What caused problems and why?**

Step 4

Concentrate on the questions your group members write, rather than covering the questions in the session. Collect the slips of paper after your group members are finished writing their questions. Then have group members form teams of four or five. Divide the slips of paper among the teams. Instruct each team to prepare a brief talk-show skit in which a panel of "prayer experts" answers the questions assigned to the team. In preparing for their presentations, encourage teams to consider how to answer each question, decide who will answer what, choose a host or moderator, and think of a relevant Scripture passage to support their answers. Give the teams a few minutes to prepare; then have them present their skits one at a time. Afterward, discuss as a group your group members' questions about prayer.

HEARD IT ALL BEFORE

LITTLE BIBLE BACKGROUND

FELLOWSHIP & WORSHIP

Step 2

Kids who've "heard it all before" may have become cynical about prayer, especially the prayer habits common among many Christians. One way to get your group members' interest and address their cynicism is to allow them to express it. Explain to them that the session is about communicating with God in prayer, but that first you're going to examine the ways different Christians go about it, at least in their public prayers. Have group members form teams. Instruct each team to brainstorm prayer caricatures—types of praying that Christians do. Examples might include the following: "preaching prayers"—prayers in which a person seems to be preaching to an audience rather than talking to God; "verbal tic prayers"— prayers in which a person continuously uses a certain word or phrase (e.g., "Dear Lord, we thank You, Lord, for today and, Lord, we ask …"); "buzzword prayers"— prayers in which a person uses all the "right" phrases, such as "pour out your blessings," "we lift up …," "touch …," etc. Teams should come up with a list of the various categories of prayers (labeling them as creatively as possible) and then write a prayer illustrating one of the categories. After the teams have read their prayers, discuss what your group members find good or bad about the prayer categories listed.

Step 4

Focus on the difficulties your group members have when it comes to praying. These might include things like finding prayer boring, having difficulty concentrating, feeling that no one is listening, fearing their prayers are repetitive, etc. Have each group member write on a slip of paper a difficulty he or she faces. Collect the slips. Then read aloud each one and ask how many other group members feel the same way. Afterward, ask volunteers to suggest ways to overcome those feelings and to pray more frequently, sincerely, and effectively.

Step 3

Some of your group members may not be very familiar with the topic of prayer. It might be helpful to begin this step by finding what they do know and what they want to know. Then you can let these needs drive the session. On the board, write three column headings: "What we *know*," "What we *want* to know," and "What we *learned*." Begin by listing all the things your group members know (or think they know) about prayer. (At this point, as group members tell you what they know, don't judge whether they are right or wrong.) Next, have them list what they want to know about prayer. Assign the passages on Repro Resource 2 to pairs or small groups and have them search their passages for answers to the questions they listed. (You may want to use the Repro Resource as a guide or supplement.) Give the pairs/small groups a few minutes to work; then have them share their answers. List these answers under the "What we learned" heading.

Step 4

If you used the "Little Bible Background" option for Step 3, review the list of questions concerning prayer under the "What we *want* to know" heading. Focus on the questions that were not answered in the Matthew and Philippians passages. If all of the questions were answered, have group members think of additional questions raised by the new things they learned about prayer. Using a concordance and your own Bible knowledge, help the kids find passages that answer their remaining questions.

Step 1

Distribute slips of paper and pencils. Have group members pair off. Instruct the members of each pair to interview each other and then write a three-sentence description of the other person based on the interview. Collect the slips of paper. Read the descriptions and see if the rest of the group can guess who is being described. When all the slips have been read, discuss which ones were easiest to guess and why. Use the activity to lead in to a discussion of the importance of communication.

Step 5

Close the session with a worship time that focuses on prayer. Encourage group members to think of several songs that have to do with prayer or communicating with God. Some examples are "Sweet Hour of Prayer," "I Love You, Lord," and the "Alleluia Song" (especially the verse, "Lord, we thank You"). Have individuals or small groups pick out a passage from the session's Bible study that they found especially meaningful. Sing one of the songs, have several kids share their passages, sing another song, share more passages, and so on. After singing the last song, close in prayer.

Step 4

After discussing the anonymous questions group members have written, choose one or two questions that are raising differing opinions. (You may want to choose a difficult question and a "less significant" one. For example: "Does God always answer prayer?" and "Do you have to close your eyes when you pray?") Have group members form two teams. The teams will debate each question. Assign one team to argue for the "yes" point of view for each question; assign the other team to present the "no" point of view.

Step 5

As a group, discuss ways to communicate other than by spoken words (actions, writing letters, etc.). List the different ways on the board as they are named. Then have each group member choose one of the ways listed on the board in communicating with God. Explain that the method group members choose will serve as a "nonverbal prayer" to God. Some may choose to write a letter to Him; others may choose to write a poem; still others may choose to draw a picture. Give group members a few minutes to work; then ask for volunteers to share their work with the rest of the group.

Step 1

You'll need a whistle for this activity. Clear a large space in your meeting area so that group members can move freely. Explain that you will give an instruction, such as "jog"; when you do, group members should follow the instruction until you blow the whistle. Group members must count the number of blasts on the whistle and form groups with that number of people in them. For example, group members may be jogging when you blow the whistle three times. They should then get into groups of three. Depending on the number of group members, not everyone will be able to get into groups of three. Those who are left over are out of the game. Continue giving commands such as jump, hop on one foot, jog backward, crawl, etc., and blowing the whistle a different number of times. After playing for a while, stop and discuss the importance of listening to the message and of communicating clearly while forming groups.

Step 2

Get your group members thinking about difficult communication by having pairs roleplay conversations between a guy and a girl. One partner should play the girl's part and the other the guy's. They should script a phone call or a situation at school or church in which the guy is trying to let the girl know that he likes her. Those group members who play the guy should think about approaches, lines, and casual ways to let the girl know how they feel. Those group members who play the girl should decide whether they're going to make the conversation tough or easy on the guy. Afterward, compare the conversations to talking to God. Talk about how nervousness, uncertainty of what to say, and uncertainty of the response can affect both conversations.

Step 1

Have group members form pairs. Give each pair a small object (not necessarily identical), such as a matchbook, marble, game token, or toothpick. (Make sure that pairs can tell their objects apart.) One person from each pair will leave to hide the object somewhere outside of the room (no more than two minutes away). The "hiders" will then draw a map to the object. They may draw pictures on the map, but may not write any words. Also, they may not talk to their partners at all. The partners, using only the map, will attempt to find the object. The first pair to bring its retrieved object to you wins. If you have time, have the partners switch roles. Afterward, have partners discuss any difficulties they encountered and whether they found the game easy or hard, and why. Discuss the importance of communication.

Step 5

Wrap up the session with a game that requires communication. Have group members form a circle. (If your group is very large, have them divide into smaller teams to form their circles.) Have kids stand in their circle shoulder to shoulder, hands stretched out to the middle; then have them grab a couple of hands. Make sure they don't hold both hands of the same person or hold hands with the people next to them. When they have grabbed hands, instruct them to "unknot" themselves—without letting go of each others' hands—so that they end up in a circle still holding hands. The activity will take a lot of communication and cooperation.

Step 1

Before the session make a list of common sayings, such as "A good man is hard to find" or "He who laughs last, laughs best." Write these on separate slips of paper and bring them to the session along with a stack of old magazines and scissors. Have group members form pairs. Give each pair a slip of paper, several magazines, and scissors. Explain that the members of each pair will have to "write" their saying using only pictures cut from the magazines (no words). The rest of the group will then try to guess the saying. For example, for "good" a pair might cut out a picture of something that looks good (perhaps a dessert). "Man" would be pretty easy to represent. The object is to see how long it takes the group to guess each pair's message. Keep track of which pair's saying is guessed the fastest. Afterward, discuss why that saying was guessed so quickly. (Some people might have had easier sayings, some might have had more useful pictures in their magazines, and so on.) Discuss how communication can be easy or difficult, but is always important.

Step 4

Play a recording of Amy Grant's classic song "El Shaddai" (from the album *Age to Age*). Then ask: **Would you consider this song a prayer? Why or why not? What kind of emotions are being expressed in the song? How would *you* express those emotions to God? What kind of praying are you most comfortable with?**

Step 1

You can skip this first activity entirely and begin with writing letters to aliens in Step 2. Or you can shorten this activity by picking two or three of the words and having a volunteer give descriptions for each one. Follow this up with the statements in the session that introduce the importance of communication.

Step 2

Shorten this activity by having kids only *think* about the messages they would send to the aliens, rather than actually writing them. Although the activity won't be as concrete since you won't have group members' actual messages to discuss, kids should get the main idea about the difficulties and advantages of communicating with a powerful being.

Step 3

Help group members recognize that prayer to God is more than some incantational formula by having them unscramble a famous prayer (or praise) from Scripture. For example, you might write out the Lord's Prayer (Matthew 6:9b-13) phrase by phrase and scramble the words. Then have group members form teams of four to six. (You'll need a scrambled prayer for each team.) Give the members of each team a copy of the prayer and have them attempt to put the words in order. Afterward, have each team read what it has assembled. Then read the actual prayer from Scripture. Ask: **Since many of your prayers are not assembled like the prayer in Scripture, does that mean your prayers are wrong?** After the discussion, reiterate that prayer is not a predetermined formula, but talking to God from what you know, feel, or need. If your group is already familiar with the Lord's Prayer, use Mary's Magnificat (Luke 1:46b-55) or Moses' Song (Exodus 15:1b-18).

Step 5

Communicate to your urban teens that "God understands 'Yo!'" Some adolescents who are unchurched are often hesitant to pray because they believe they must use certain words to get to God. Help them see the falsity of this idea. Say: **God both speaks and understands "Yo." So don't be afraid to pray, even if it is in slang.** Afterward, have each group member write a prayer to God in slang and read it aloud.

Step 2

Instead of having group members write to the alien beings, which some high schoolers may not relish, have them concentrate on the difficulties of prayer. Have group members form teams. Give each team a poster board and markers. In the middle of the poster board, team members should write the word *prayer* and circle it. Then have them brainstorm all the obstacles to prayer or difficulties in praying that they can think of. They can add these ideas to their posters as branches coming off the prayer circle. If some of the difficulties suggest related difficulties, they could have a second tier of branches. When the teams are finished, have them display their posters. Then explain that the rest of the session will concentrate on the Bible's guidelines for helping us overcome prayer difficulties.

Step 4

After group members turn in the slips with their questions about prayer, divide the questions among pairs (or teams, if you have a large group). The pairs should read the questions and, pretending that they are advice columnists, answer them. (To save time, you might have each pair answer only one question.) Encourage the pairs to include Scripture in their replies and to give practical suggestions. For example, if someone asks, "How often should I pray?" they could answer that the Bible tells us to pray without ceasing, and then suggest some practical times and places: when you get up or go to bed, at meals, while walking to class, during a study break, and so on. After a few minutes, have the pairs share their questions and responses. Get the rest of the group to suggest additional Scripture passages or practical advice.

Step 3

Make an extra copy of "Prayer Specifications" (Repro Resource 2). Cut it apart so that each of the nine questions is on a separate slip of paper. Have group members form teams of three or four. Instruct the teams to alternate taking one slip of paper until all of the questions have been distributed. Then give a whole copy of Repro Resource 2 to each team. Have the teams read through the Bible passages listed on the sheet to find the answer(s) to their question(s). Instruct the teams to be prepared to share their information with the rest of the group.

Step 4

Before asking group members to write down their questions about prayer, have them consider some of the impressions they've had of prayer since they were small children. Ask: **What is the first prayer you remember saying or hearing? What were your ideas and questions about prayer when you were very young?** As group members think about their early childhood experiences involving prayer, ask them to write some questions from that very young point of view. Ask: **If you were only five years old, what question might you ask about prayer?**

Date Used:

Approx.
Time

Step 1: Guess What! _____
o Small Group
o Large Group
o Fellowship & Worship
o Mostly Guys
o Extra Fun
o Media
o Short Meeting Time
Things needed:

**Step 2: Adventurous
Communicators** _____
o Extra Action
o Heard It All Before
o Mostly Guys
o Short Meeting Time
o Combined Junior High/High School
Things needed:

**Step 3: Communication
Clarified** _____
o Extra Action
o Little Bible Background
o Urban
o Sixth Grade
Things needed:

Step 4: Hows and Whys _____
o Small Group
o Large Group
o Heard It All Before
o Little Bible Background
o Mostly Girls
o Media
o Combined Junior High/High School
o Sixth Grade
Things needed:

Step 5: We Have a Prayer _____
o Fellowship & Worship
o Mostly Girls
o Extra Fun
o Urban
Things needed:

3 How to Read the Bible

YOUR GOALS FOR THIS SESSION:

Choose one or more

☐ To help kids recognize that reading the Bible can benefit them.

☐ To help kids understand how Bible study can change their lives.

☐ To help kids make a commitment to study God's Word regularly or to make a change in their lives because of something they found in Scripture.

☐ Other _____

Your Bible Base:

Psalm 119:97-120
Ephesians 4:29-32

STEP
1

The Wrong Instructions

(Needed: Copies of Repro Resource 3, paper cup, masking tape or string, paper clips)

Before the session, make enough copies of the top half of "2 Games" (Repro Resource 3) so that all but two of your group members will have one. Then make two copies of the bottom half of Repro Resource 3. Mix the sheets together in one stack, but make sure you put the two bottom halves near the top of the stack so that two group members will be sure to get them when you pass out the sheets.

You'll also need to make a circle on your floor using masking tape or string. The circle should be about six feet in diameter. Place a paper cup in the center of the circle.

When group members arrive, give each one ten paper clips and a copy of Repro Resource 3. (Pay attention to who receives the two bottom halves of the sheet.) Then say: **To begin today's session, we're going to play a game called "Clip Toss." The instructions for the game are on the sheet I just gave you. Read them over carefully.**

Give group members a minute to read their instructions. Then remind them that they are not to talk at all during the game. When you're ready, have them begin.

Let the game go on for a couple minutes, or until group members begin to lose interest. Then say: **Time's up. Who's our winner? Who knocked the cup over the most times?**

Most kids will protest because knocking the cup over wasn't what they were instructed to do. After the turmoil dies down a bit, have someone read his or her directions. Then have someone else read the other set of directions.

Say: **You were supposed to be trying to knock the cup over. Some of you must not have had the right instructions.**

How did not having the right instructions affect how you played the game? (Responses might include "I was trying to do the wrong thing"; "I didn't know what I was supposed to do to win.")

In what other areas of our lives do we rely on instructions? (Learning to drive a car, learning a skill or a trade, learning to play sports, cooking, assembling things, etc.)

What would it be like to try to live our lives without having any instructions? (It would be tough. We'd mess up all the time. We wouldn't know what we were supposed to do.)

Explain: **As Christians, the Bible is our instruction book for life. It doesn't give a rule for every little thing, but it gives us principles to live by. It helps us know what the purpose of life really is. Without the Bible, we'd have trouble figuring out the right directions for life. But we can only learn from the Bible if we read it. In this session, we're going to be talking about what we have to gain from the Bible and how important it is to our lives.**

STEP 2

What Good Is It?

(Needed: Bibles, wastebasket, foam ball, paper, pencils, prize [optional])

Have group members form two teams. Explain: **We're going to play a Bible study game. I'm going to give each team five minutes to study a passage of Scripture and come up with a list of benefits for studying the Bible, based on that passage. For each benefit you come up with, your team gets one shot at the wastebasket with the foam ball. The team that hits the most shots wins.**

Distribute paper and pencils to each team. Explain that, for every benefit the teams list, they must also give a Scripture reference to back it up. Announce that the reference is Psalm 119:97-120, and have the teams begin their search.

When the five minutes are up, have a spokesperson from each team read off the team's list, including the references. Have all group members check the reference for each benefit, making sure that each one is legitimate. (An added benefit of this part of the activity is solidifying each benefit in group members' minds as they check them.)

After you've verified the benefits, let the teams take their shots at the wastebasket. Set it up about ten feet away, and let the teams go at it. Remind group members that their teams get one shot per verified benefit they listed. Have teams alternate shots, and don't let any team member shoot twice until all other team members have had a shot.

When the shooting is done, declare a winner. You may want to give a prize, a round of applause, or some other form of recognition to the winning team.

Afterward, discuss: **How does God's Word make us wiser**

O P T I O N S

LITTLE BIBLE BACKGROUND

MOSTLY GIRLS

MEDIA

SHORT MEETING TIME

URBAN

JR. HIGH / HIGH SCHOOL COMBINED

than our enemies? (It helps us know right from wrong. It keeps us from doing dumb things that will hurt ourselves.)

What does it mean that God's Word is a lamp unto our path? (It helps us see the "path" we should follow. It keeps us from falling into bad stuff.)

How is God's Word the joy of our hearts? (It reminds us of all God has done for us. It makes us happy to know that God loves us.)

What hope does God's Word give us? (It gives us the hope of heaven, knowing that God will take care of us for eternity.)

How can God's promise keep us going? (It lets us know God is on our side. We know He'll be there no matter what happens to us.)

Say: **There are a lot of good reasons to read and study the Bible. We've just looked at a few of them. Now we're going to look at a passage of Scripture to see how it can help us in our everyday lives.**

STEP 3

Three Tough Questions

(Needed: Chalkboard and chalk or newsprint and marker, Bibles, paper, pencils)

Say: **To help you discover how this next passage of Scripture can help us in our everyday lives, I'm going to give you three questions to think about as you read through the passage.** Write the three questions on the board as you name them.

- **What does this passage say?**
- **What does it mean to me?**
- **What am I going to do about it?**

Have group members form teams of three. Distribute paper and pencils to each team. Instruct the teams to look up Ephesians 4:29-32, asking each of the three questions for each verse. Go around to the teams as they work, helping them when they get stuck and encouraging them to be specific in their answers—especially for the third question.

When the teams are finished, have them share the insights they found. Don't let any one team dominate the discussion, and make sure each team contributes something.

Use the following suggestions to supplement the teams' responses.
Verse 29
What does this passage say? (We should not say unwholesome things

to other people. Instead, we should say things that build them up.)

What does it mean to me? (I should stop making fun of other people and begin complimenting and encouraging them.)

What am I going to do about it? (Instead of making fun of the guy who sits next to me in history class, I'm going to be nice to him.)

Verse 30

What does this passage say? (As Christians, we should not do things that cause the Holy Spirit to be grieved.)

What does it mean to me? (I should identify the things I do in my life that cause the Holy Spirit grief, and eliminate them.)

What am I going to do about it? (I'm going to cut down on my "unwholesome talk—that means I'm going to try to stop swearing, gossiping, and cutting down others.)

Verse 31

What does this passage say? (As Christians, we should eliminate bitterness, rage, anger, and slander from our lives.)

What does it mean to me? (I'm going to have to be more aware of my bitterness, anger, and tendency to slander.)

What am I going to do about it? (Catch myself when I start to say something out of bitterness or anger, or when I start to say something negative about someone.)

Verse 32

What does this passage say? (As Christians, we should be be kind, compassionate, and willing to forgive others.)

What does it mean to me? (I should show kindness and compassion not only to my friends, but also to people I don't particularly like. Also, I shouldn't hold grudges against other people.)

What am I going to do about it? (Make an effort to stick up for someone who's being picked on at school. Listen to someone who's having problems in his or her life. Take the first step in making up with someone I've been fighting with.)

Say: **There are thousands and thousands of verses in the Bible. Look at how many practical tips we got from just four of them. Imagine how many more there are just waiting to be found.**

Some people say that studying the Bible is difficult—and sometimes it can be. But there many things you can do—like using the three questions we just discussed—to make Bible study more interesting and personal.

O P T I O N S

EXTRA ACTION

LARGE GROUP

HEARD IT ALL BEFORE

LITTLE BIBLE BACKGROUND

MOSTLY GUYS

MEDIA

SIXTH GRADE

STEP

4

Getting Going

(Needed: Slips of paper, pencils)

Distribute slips of paper to your group members. Explain: **We've talked about how Bible study can benefit us—but the hard part is getting started. Reading the Bible doesn't mean you have to sit down with it an hour a day and read it through from cover to cover. But you might be able to find ten minutes two or three times a week to see what God has to say to you. You could even use the same three questions we just used to help you learn from what you read.**

What did your team find in Scripture today that you said you're going to do something about? Group members should be able to answer from the third question in their team study of Ephesians 4:29-32.

Think about how your life could improve if even one or two times a week you found a principle or teaching in the Bible to help you. On your slip of paper, write something that you're going to commit yourself to. It may be something you found in the Ephesians passage, or it may be a commitment simply to study the Bible on a regular basis. Don't make the commitment too tough, or you may just be setting yourself up for failure. Start out small and follow through on your commitment. Then maybe you can increase your commitment as you find how much your original commitment has helped you.

After group members have written their commitments on their slips of paper, close the session with prayer. Pray that God will help your group members follow through on the commitments they've made, and that they will become regular studiers of His Word. As group members leave, encourage them to take their slips of paper home and put them in their Bibles as reminders of their commitments.

2 GAMES

CLIP TOSS

The object of this game is to get as many paper clips as possible into the paper cup. You must stand outside the circle to toss the paper clips. If someone knocks the cup over, only that person can enter the circle to stand it back up. You may pick up and re-use tossed paper clips, if you can reach them without any part of your body touching the floor inside the circle. You may not speak at any time during the game. Keep track of how many paper clips you get in the cup.

CLIP TOSS

The object of this game is to knock over the paper cup as many times as possible. You must stand outside the circle to toss the paper clips. If you knock over the cup, only you can enter the circle to stand it back up. You may pick up and re-use tossed paper clips, if you can reach them without any part of your body touching the floor inside the circle. You may not speak at any time during the game. Keep track of how many times you knock over the paper cup.

Step 1

If you're looking for a more active opener, try the following idea. Before the session, you'll need to prepare two index cards. One card should say "Your goal is to shoot as many paper wads as possible into the trash can." The other card should say "Your goal is to prevent paper wads from being thrown into the trash can." To begin the session, have group members form two teams. Give each team one of the cards. Then set out a supply of paper wads and let the teams go about carrying out the instructions on their cards. Encourage the teams to use creative strategy in playing the game. After a few minutes, stop the action. Then announce: **If there are twenty-five paper wads in the trash can, everyone in the group will win a prize.** Ideally, there won't be twenty-five paper wads in the can. If that's the case, one team will probably blame the other for preventing them from shooting the paper wads. Use the last three questions in Step 1 to discuss the activity.

Step 3

Have group members form four teams. Assign each team one of the verses in Ephesians 4:29-32. Instruct the teams to look up their assigned verse and answer the three questions on the board. Then have them come up with brief skits illustrating one thing a person could do to put the verse into practice. An effective way for teams to do this would be to create "before-and-after" skits, demonstrating how a person might react to a situation before reading the verse, and how he or she might act after reading the verse. For example, one skit might be set in a school cafeteria setting. In the "before" segment, a character might be making fun of or gossiping about someone else. In the "after" segment, he or she might invite the other person to sit with him or her or may say nice things instead of gossiping. After each team performs its skit, have the rest of the group members suggest other ways to put the verse into practice.

Step 1

A small group will allow you the opportunity to have group members share some personal experiences in which not following instructions or following the wrong instructions led to trouble. For instance, some group members might talk about a time when they got lost because of poor directions. Others might talk about a time when they couldn't assemble something because they misread the instructions. Still others might talk about a time when they flunked a test because they didn't do what the teacher said. You may want to share an example from your own life to get things started. Follow up the sharing time with a discussion on the importance of directions—of having them, understanding them, and following them.

Step 4

If your small group is closely knit, you may want to wrap up the session with a time of group prayer. Before the prayer time, ask group members to silently make a commitment based on one of the Scripture passages they read during the session. Then have group members stand and form a circle for prayer. If you think your group members would be comfortable with it, instruct each one of them to pray (perhaps just a sentence prayer) for the person on his or her right, that the person will follow through on his or her commitment. If your group members wouldn't feel comfortable about praying aloud, have them pray silently.

Step 1

You could speed up the "clip toss" game for a large group by having group members form more than one circle and by using more than one cup. Or you could try a different game to get all of your group members interacting. Have group members form a circle and hold hands. Gently squeeze the hand of the person to your left. He or she should then do the same thing to the person on his or her left, and so on. Once the squeeze has been passed around the circle a few times, add another dimension by saying "Aah" to the person to your left. (He or she will then pass it on.) After a while say "Ooh" to the person on your right. (Somebody in the circle will get caught between the "Aah" and the "Ooh.") Add additional variations as necessary. After you've played for a while and have everyone entirely confused, stop. Point out that the game required group members to follow directions (or someone's lead). Discuss why following directions is sometimes difficult. List some other areas in life in which we need to follow instructions. Then point out that the Bible gives us instructions to follow.

Step 3

Modify this step in one or more of the following ways. (1) Have group members form teams of five, rather than three. (2) If you have adult volunteers, ask each one lead a smaller discussion group composed of several teams. This way all the teams will be able to respond to each verse. Kids may also be more willing to share in smaller groups. (3) Rather than having all of the teams say something for each verse, have only two teams per verse share their responses. Assign the verses in such a way that each team discusses at least one.

Step 1
Get group members thinking about the things that make them feel cynical or bored about studying the Bible by having them come up with a list of ten reasons *not* to read the Bible. (Explain that they don't necessarily have to agree with the reasons, but they should give reasons that people are likely to use.) Begin by turning off the lights and shining a flashlight around the room at group members. When the "spotlight" stops on someone, that person has to give a reason not to read the Bible. List the reason on the board. Keep going until you have at least ten reasons. If you get more then ten, have group members choose the top ten once the lights are on. After you go over the list, explain to group members that in this session, they will see what the Bible has to say to defend itself against these charges.

Step 3
Group members who've "heard it all before" may be used to giving "standard" answers to the question "What does this Bible passage mean to me?" So for the Bible study activity, substitute a question like "How would you explain this passage—without using 'typical' Christian expressions and phrases—to someone who's never read the Bible before?" for the "What does it mean to me?" question.

Step 2
Introduce Psalm 119 by explaining that it is a poem in praise of the Scriptures and that it is written in acrostic form: each section stands for a letter of the Hebrew alphabet and each line in that section begins with that letter. Point out that the psalm makes an analogy between living and walking on a path. The writer wants to walk the path of righteousness—that is, to live in a way that pleases God; he wants to see the path clearly and to avoid taking wrong turns. You might also explain that "dross" refers to the impurities contained in metals. In the refining process in which the ore is melted, the dross rises to the top where it is skimmed off and thrown away, leaving only the pure metal.

Step 3
At the beginning of this step, explain that you are going to demonstrate to group members a simple method they can use to read and study the Bible. After writing the three questions on the board, read the passage in Ephesians. Then, since this study method will probably be new to some of your group members, model the method for them by answering the questions for the first verse. Explain what it says, what it means to you, and what you will do about it. Be personal, honest, and specific. Help your group members see that how you read the Bible can make a difference in your life.

Step 1
Get group members warmed up and interacting by playing a game in which they have to think fast and follow directions. Clear a space in your meeting area so that kids can move about freely. Let them mill around for a minute or so; then give a group-forming command, such as **Form groups of four.** When kids have formed groups of four, say: **Now quickly share with the members of your group the last Bible verse or passage of Scripture you memorized.** After a minute or two, give another group-forming command (perhaps **Form an odd-numbered group** or **Form a group that is a multiple of three**). Here are some other instructions you might use once group members have formed their groups:
• **Share your favorite book of the Bible and explain why it's your favorite.**
• **Share one question you've always had about the Bible.**
• **Share your favorite miracle in the Bible and explain why it's your favorite.**

Use the activity to lead into a discussion of the importance of following instructions.

Step 4
Create a short worship service focused on God's Word. Step 2 showed some of the ways that God's Word benefits us: it gives us wisdom, direction, joy, hope, and promise. For your service, have group members find at least one verse for each of these five categories. For example, for "promise," you might use "In my Father's house are many rooms. . . . I am going there to prepare a place for you" (John 14:2). Conduct the worship time by announcing the category, perhaps with prayer ("We thank You, Lord, that Your Word gives us wisdom. . . ."); then have volunteers read aloud the appropriate passage(s).

Step 2

Have group members form teams to compete in the Bible study game. Have each team study the assigned Scripture passage and list as many benefits as they can of studying the Bible. If possible, bring in several foam balls. Then give each team just 30 seconds to attempt its earned shots with the balls. (Setting a short time limit should increase the excitement level of the activity.) Keep a tally on the board of each team's score. If you have a tie score at the end of the contest, have the tied teams compete in a 30-second play-off, in which each team gets 30 seconds to make as many shots as possible.

Step 4

On the board, list group members' responses to question #3 in Step 3. At this point in the session, ask group members to identify which items on the board would be somewhat easy to do and which would be pretty difficult. Then ask: Do you think the Bible is a difficult book to live by? Why or why not? What makes the Bible such an important book to use as a guide for our lives? Instruct group members to choose one of the responses written on the board as a personal challenge. Have them write that challenge on their slip of paper.

Step 1

Get group members thinking about following instructions by playing a game of "horse" (or "pig," if time is limited). You will need a basketball and a hoop or a wastebasket and a beanbag or foam rubber ball. Explain that the object is not only to make the basket but also to create a series of moves that each person must follow. Encourage group members to be creative. For example, someone might start at the free throw line, bounce twice, scratch his head, spin around three times, and sink the shot off the backboard. Afterward, discuss following the "instructions" in the game. Ask: **Was it easy or difficult? Did the "instructions" matter much in this game?** Then discuss other kinds of instructions—which ones matter and why.

Step 3

Discussing practical ways of changing our behavior to live more like Christ provides you with a good opportunity to talk about sex, something that is often on the minds of junior high guys. Have your group members think about locker room conversations, the jokes they tell and laugh at, what they say about women, what they think about them, what movies and videos they watch, etc. Encourage them to find an example of how the teaching in each verse applies to this area of their lives. For example, the Holy Spirit is grieved not only by what we do but also by what we think.

Step 1

Have group members form three or four teams for a relay game. Players from each team must balance an eraser (or some other object) on their head (without using their hands to steady it) and walk across the room. When they reach the other side, they will grab the eraser, hop back to the line, and give the eraser to a teammate. The first team to send all of its players across and back wins. The catch is that you will give one of the teams different instructions. Allow players on that team to hold the eraser in place with their hands. This way they should be able to walk faster and their team should win. When the other teams complain that they had to balance their erasers, tell them they must have had the wrong instructions. Then use the questions in the session to introduce the topic of instructions.

Step 4

Wrap up the session with a fun and delicious way of reinforcing the benefits of following good directions. Choose some kind of snack that requires people to put something together (peanut butter and jelly sandwiches, ice-cream sundaes, decorated cookies, etc.). Have group members write directions for this activity on slips of paper. Collect the slips and pick out several of them. Ask for volunteers to follow the instructions on the slips. As you watch, make sure the person follows exactly what's written in the instructions. For example, suppose the directions for making a peanut butter and jelly sandwich said, "Spread peanut butter on two slices of bread"; the volunteer should spread peanut butter on *both* sides of each slice, since the directions don't specify. After the volunteers have followed the directions (and probably made an interesting mess), have the rest of the group members make their own snacks.

Step 2

Before the game, play a recording of Amy Grant's song "Thy Word" (from the album *Straight Ahead*). Then ask: **How does this song describe God's Word?** (As "a lamp unto my feet and a light unto my path.") **What do you think each of these images is referring to?** After a couple of group members have responded, point out that the song is based on Psalm 119:97-120. Then continue the activity as described in the session.

Step 3

Before the session, record several people reading the Ephesians 4 passage from various versions and paraphrases of the Bible. Make sure you include the following: King James Version, New International Version, New American Standard Bible, the Living Bible, and the Good News Bible (as well as any other translations or paraphrases you'd like to use). Play the tape for your group members and have them rank the versions according to which ones they'd most prefer to use in studying Scripture. Point out that there are a number of different Bible translations and paraphrases for us to choose from. Encourage group members to find one they feel comfortable with. If possible, you might want to have several different Bibles available for group members to use during the session—especially for the section in which they answer the three questions on the board.

Step 1

Either skip this step and begin the session with Step 2 or try the following shorter activity. Challenge your group members to come up with an area of life for which there aren't instructions. Group members may be able to think of some area, but along the way they'll realize that much of what we do, we do because we've been instructed how to do it (even simple things like brushing teeth, tying shoes, or washing hands). Get them thinking about the necessity of instructions for many of life's activities.

Step 2

You can shorten this activity considerably by skipping the basket-shooting competition. If you'd still like to give group members some added incentive for creating their lists, you could simply award prizes to the team that lists the most benefits.

Step 1

At the beginning of the session, it might be a good idea to find out what your group members know (or think they know) about the Bible. Ask: **What instructions are in the Bible for us?** Write all of your group members' responses, whether they're right or wrong, on the board. Then go through the list and identify which are correct. Then ask the following question and announce that you will award prizes to the people who answer correctly. **Which of the following pieces of advice comes from the Bible?**
(a) A penny saved is a penny earned.
(b) We have nothing to fear but fear itself.
(c) Love your enemies and pray for those who persecute you.
(d) Ask not what your country can do for you, but what you can do for your country.
(e) Early to bed, early to rise, make a man healthy, wealthy, and wise.
(f) God helps those who help themselves.
Announce that the correct answer is "c" (Matthew 5:44). Award prizes. Then point out that knowing moral adages is not enough; God wants us to be able to recognize and live out that which comes directly from the Bible, lest we follow incorrect instructions.

Step 2

Another option with the foam balls is to have group members stand in a circle, equal distance from the trash can. Ask group members ten questions from Scripture. The first person to answer correctly will get to shoot the ball at the trash can. If the person hits the shot, he or she gets to move one step closer to the trash can. The person who hits the most shots wins. Obviously, those who know Scripture best and have the best aim will have best results. Point out that memorizing Scripture won't *move us forward* in life unless it is *accurately tossed* (implemented) toward and for God.

Step 1
Get group members thinking about the different attitudes that kids at their schools (and perhaps they themselves) have about the Bible. Have group members form pairs. Distribute paper and pencils to each pair. Instruct the pairs to list the attitudes they think of. Encourage the pairs to consider whether the kids at school would find the Bible relevant, important, interesting, true, or understandable. For each attitude, have them write an attitude-revealing name and brief description. You might get them started with these examples: Peter Practical, who thinks the Bible was written too long ago to be relevant today; Nancy Know-Little, who has heard of the Bible and thinks it has something to do with Jesus and Moses; Chris Comic Strip, who thinks the Bible is boring because it has too many words and no pictures. (For fun, you might have junior high kids write high schoolers' attitudes and vice versa.) Afterward, have the pairs share their lists; briefly discuss the attitudes that are named. Then explain that in this session, you're going to see what the Bible says about itself.

Step 2
After reading the passages and coming up with a list of benefits, have group members apply the benefits to one of the caricatures they came up with in the "Combined Junior High/High School" option for Step 1. (You'll need to have group members pair up as they did in Step 1.) For example, for Peter Practical, they might explain that God's Word is a lamp; it shows us how to avoid trouble, so it's very practical—even today. Give the pairs a few minutes to work. Then have them explain their applications by either roleplaying a conversation with caricature or completing the following statement: "Although some people think _____, the truth is that the Bible _____."

Step 3
Rather than having all of your sixth graders work on all four of the verses, have half of the teams focus on Ephesians 4:29, 30 and the other teams focus on Ephesians 4:31, 32. Afterward, have the teams share their information. Instruct group members to take notes on what is said about the verses they did not look up.

Step 4
Go back over the responses group members gave to question #3 in Step 3. Write these responses on the board. Then distribute slips of paper and pencils. Instruct group members to choose one of the responses on the board as a commitment to follow through on.

Date Used:

Approx.
Time

Step 1: The Wrong Instructions _____
o Extra Action
o Small Group
o Large Group
o Heard It All Before
o Fellowship & Worship
o Mostly Guys
o Extra Fun
o Short Meeting Time
o Urban
o Combined Junior High/High School
Things needed:

Step 2: What Good Is It? _____
o Little Bible Background
o Mostly Girls
o Media
o Short Meeting Time
o Urban
o Combined Junior High/High School
Things needed:

Step 3: Three Tough Questions _____
o Extra Action
o Large Group
o Heard It All Before
o Little Bible Background
o Mostly Guys
o Media
o Sixth Grade
Things needed:

Step 4: Getting Going _____
o Small Group
o Fellowship & Worship
o Mostly Girls
o Extra Fun
o Sixth Grade
Things needed:

How to Fight Temptation

YOUR GOALS FOR THIS SESSION:

Choose one or more

☐ To help kids recognize how tempting temptations can be.

☐ To help kids understand how God can help them in tempting situations.

☐ To help kids begin to combat the temptations they face with the help of Scripture.

☐ Other _____

_____

Your Bible Base:

I Corinthians 10:1-13
Hebrews 4:14-16
I John 1:5—2:2

Tempted!

(Needed: A tempting treat for your group members)

Bring to the session a tasty, tempting treat for your group members. Make sure you bring enough for everyone. Set the treat in an obvious place in your meeting room. Don't say anything about it to group members as they enter. If they ask about it, try to ignore them. If they persist, tell them to wait. If they just start digging in, don't say anything.

After everyone has arrived, have group members sit down around the treat. Take care of any announcements or business you have, or make small talk for a couple of minutes.

Then ask: **How many of you were tempted to sample this treat?**

How many of you *did* sample this treat?

For those of you who didn't, what kept you from sampling the treat? (Some might say they were waiting for you to tell them when to eat it. Others might say they weren't hungry or they don't like that kind of treat.)

If your group members ate the treat before your meeting started, gather them together and ask: **How many of you gave in to the temptation to eat the treat?**

Why didn't you wait? (Some might say the treat looked or smelled too good to resist. Others might say they just assumed it was OK to eat the treats.)

What made it hard to resist the temptation? (Some might say they ate the treats because everyone else was eating them. Others might say they were afraid none of the treats would be left if they'd waited.)

Say: **Giving in to this temptation wasn't (or wouldn't be) a really big deal. The treat was intended for you, and the only harmful thing about it is probably the sugar. But other temptations are much more dangerous.**

What are some of the major temptations junior highers face in today's society? (Drugs, drinking, sex, vandalism, cheating, etc.)

What makes these temptations so attractive? (They make you feel good. Many other kids are doing them. Doing them can help you fit in with other people. Temptations like cheating can help you "get ahead.")

What might be some of the negative results of giving in to these temptations? (You could get addicted to drugs or alcohol. Getting drunk can make you really sick. If you get caught, there's big trouble.)

Say: **Temptations are often tough to resist. Something bad can look really attractive at times. But most of the time, giving in to temptation can be really bad for us. In this session, we're going to look at some ways to avoid giving in to some of these bad temptations. But first, let's give in to a good temptation and finish off this treat!** Let group members eat the treat if they haven't already done so.

STEP
2

Book Review

(Needed: Bibles, a copy of Repro Resource 4, microphone [optional])

Explain that in this activity group members will read through a passage of Scripture, and then be interviewed about it. Ask for a volunteer to be the interviewer. Then have the rest of the group members form three teams. Give the interviewer a copy of "The Interview" (Repro Resource 4) to read over. Have him or her prepare to play the part while the teams are working.

Assign each team one of the following passages: I Corinthians 10:1-13; Hebrews 4:14-16; or I John 1:5–2:2. Instruct the teams to read through their passages a couple of times and prepare themselves to answer questions based on the passages. Give the teams about five minutes to study the passages.

While the teams are studying, encourage your interviewer to really get into his or her part, and perform it like Phil Donahue, Oprah Winfrey, or some other TV interviewer. Encourage him or her to press for specific, helpful answers to the questions.

After five minutes, have the interviewer start with the questions from the script. For effect, you might want to give him or her a microphone to use for the interviews. As he or she asks questions, be sure the other group members give good answers. They may use their Bibles for help if they need to. You may want to ask follow-up questions if necessary, or encourage your interviewer to press harder for answers.

Use the following information as a guideline as you press for more information from group members.

OPTIONS

SMALL GROUP

LARGE GROUP

HEARD IT ALL BEFORE

LITTLE BIBLE BACKGROUND

SHORT MEETING TIME

URBAN

SIXTH GRADE

1 Corinthians 10:1-13

What kinds of things does this author say we aren't supposed to do? (Set our hearts on evil things, like the children of Israel did; practice idolatry; commit sexual immorality; test the Lord; grumble.)

Why did some of the bad things mentioned by this author happen? (As examples and warnings for us.)

What does the author say we're supposed to be careful about? (We should be careful that we don't fall when we think we're standing firm.)

Why is it possible to avoid giving in to temptation—no matter what the temptation is? (God will not let us be tempted beyond what we can bear. He will provide a way out for us.)

Who can help us when we're facing a tough temptation? (God.)

Hebrews 4:14-16

According to this author, how does Jesus feel about our weaknesses? (He sympathizes with us, because He knows what it's like to be tempted.)

What does it mean that Jesus has been tempted in every way just as we are? (When He was on earth, Jesus faced the same kinds of temptation that we face.)

How did Jesus do in facing temptation when He was on earth? (He never once gave in to temptation. He remained sinless.)

How can we get help when we face temptation? (We can approach Jesus' throne—through prayer—and receive mercy and grace to help us in our time of need.)

1 John 1:5–2:2

What happens when we do what's right? (We have fellowship with other believers, and the blood of Jesus purifies us from all sin.)

What if we don't tell anybody and pretend everything is OK when we give in to temptation? (We are lying, and are not living by the truth. We deceive ourselves.)

What happens if we admit we've messed up and ask for forgiveness? (We will be forgiven and purified from all unrighteousness.)

What did Jesus do that makes it possible for God to forgive us? (He took upon Himself the punishment we deserved and paid the penalty for our sin by dying on the cross.)

When the interview is completed, give everyone a round of applause. Then say: **God cares about us. He knows we face temptations that are tough, and He sympathizes with us. He promises that He'll never let us get in a situation in which there's no way out. He's given us an example in Jesus to show us that we can be tempted and still not sin. If we mess up, there'll be consequences to live with, but God promises to forgive us if we admit our sin to Him. There's no need for Him to do any more than that. The rest is up to us.**

STEP
3

Personal Temptations

(Needed: Copies of Repro Resource 5, pencils, Bibles)

Have group members form pairs. Distribute copies of "Create-a-Temptation" (Repro Resource 5) and pencils to each pair. Instruct the members of each pair to work together in completing the first section of the sheet, and to work individually in responding to the last question on the sheet. Give the pairs a few minutes to work. Then go through the actions one at a time, asking the members of each pair to share what they came up with for each one.

After all the pairs have shared their ideas for a particular action, ask the following questions: **How might someone avoid giving in to this temptation?**

How might the Bible passages we've looked at today be helpful in battling this temptation?

How might Christian friends be helpful in battling this temptation?

After you've gone through all six actions on the sheet, ask volunteers to share their responses to the final question on the sheet. If no one volunteers, that's OK. Don't force anyone to share.

Afterward, say: **Temptations can be tough to resist. Sometimes bad things look like a lot of fun. But we can have a lot of fun without doing things that are displeasing to God.**

OPTIONS

EXTRA ACTION

LITTLE BIBLE BACKGROUND

MOSTLY GIRLS

MOSTLY GUYS

MEDIA

SHORT MEETING TIME

SIXTH GRADE

STEP
4

Good Clean Fun

(Needed: Chalkboard and chalk or newsprint and marker, Bibles)

Have your group members brainstorm ideas for fun things to do that don't involve giving in to bad temptations. As they suggest ideas, write them on the board.

OPTIONS

SMALL GROUP

FELLOWSHIP & WORSHIP

MOSTLY GIRLS

EXTRA FUN

URBAN

JR. HIGH HIGH SCHOOL COMBINED

After you've got a list of at least fifteen things, ask group members if they all agree that all of the things you've listed are OK. Discuss any questionable ones, letting several group members offer input.

Then say: **As you can see from this list, there are a lot of fun things to do that don't displease God. Of course, there are also a lot of things we can do that do displease God. But fortunately, as we saw earlier, God gives us help in resisting wrong actions—if we rely on Him.**

How do we rely on God to help us through temptations? (Study the Bible. Think about what God would want us to do when we make decisions. Ask for His help when we know we're going to have trouble.)

How can we help our friends resist temptations? (Be a good example. Encourage them when they're trying to do right. Try to talk them out of doing dumb things.)

Explain: **With God's help, we can resist temptations. And we can also be used by Him to help others resist temptation. So we need to be depending on Him at all times to help us make the right decisions.**

Have group members open their Bibles to one of the passages you studied today: I Corinthians 10:1-13; Hebrews 4:14-16; or I John 1:5–2:2.

Say: **As we wrap up this session, choose one part of one of these verses to hang on to as your own. It can be just a short phrase, or most of a verse. Memorize a short part of it right now, to help you face temptation in the future.**

Give group members about two minutes to find a verse segment and memorize it. Then say: **As I close our session in prayer, thank God for His Word. Consider committing yourself to God to use the bit of Scripture you've just memorized to help you resist temptation this week.**

Close your session in prayer, asking God to help your group members with the temptations they will face in the coming week.

T·H·E
INTERVIEW

Today on our book review segment we're going to be looking at a hot topic: temptation! We've got sections of three different books to look at, and a panel of experts who've studied each of these segments to help us get some answers to our questions. Would someone please read aloud I Corinthians 10:1-13?

(HAVE SOMEONE FROM THE GROUP READ THE PASSAGE.)

Thank you. Now let's dig a little bit. What kinds of things does this author say we aren't supposed to do?

Why did some of the bad things mentioned by this author happen?

What does the author say we're supposed to be careful about?

Why is it possible to avoid giving in to temptation— no matter what the temptation is?

Who can help us when we're facing a tough temptation?

Thank you very much for your input. Now let's check out what the next author has to say. Would someone please read aloud Hebrews 4:14-16?

(HAVE SOMEONE FROM THE GROUP READ THE PASSAGE.)

According to this author, how does Jesus feel about our weaknesses?

What does it mean that Jesus has been tempted in every way just as we are?

How did Jesus do in facing temptation when He was on earth?

How can we get help when we face temptation?

Sounds like there's a lot of help available when we need it. But what happens when we do good and when we mess up? Somebody read I John 1:5–2:2.

(HAVE SOMEONE FROM THE GROUP READ THE PASSAGE.)

What happens when we do what's right?

What if we don't tell anybody and pretend everything is OK when we give in to temptation?

What happens if we admit we've messed up and ask for forgiveness?

What did Jesus do that makes it possible for God to forgive us?

Thank you very much. Let's give our panel a much-deserved round of applause.

CREATE-A-TEMPTATION

For each of the following actions, draw or describe a situation in which someone might be tempted.

Drinking alcohol

Cheating at school

Doing drugs

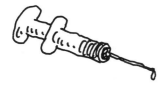

Going too far sexually

Destroying something

Stealing

Now describe a real-life situation in which you've been tempted to do something wrong.

EXTRA ACTION

Step 1
You'll need a lot of paper wads for this activity. Have group members form two teams for a "paper-wad war." Say: **The rules of the game are simple. If you're hit with a paper wad thrown by a member of the other team, you're out. The team that has the most players still in when I call time wins.** Give the teams a few minutes to build "fortresses" (using tables and chairs) and/or plan battle strategies. Then begin the game. After several group members are out, briefly stop the action. Announce: **I'm going to allow those who are out to reenter the game. However, they are all now members of Team A.** This should give Team A a decided advantage. After a few more minutes, announce that the winning team will receive prizes (perhaps cookies, candy, or some other tempting treat). When there are only three or four players left on Team B, stop the action again. Give two members of Team B an opportunity to join Team A. Then, after a few more minutes, end the game. Discuss the temptation Team B members faced when it came to joining Team A. Then lead into a discussion of everyday temptations kids face.

Step 3
Assign each pair one of the temptations on Repro Resource 5. Instruct the members of each pair to create a brief skit illustrating their assigned temptation. Encourage them to make the situation as tempting as possible. Before performing the skit, they should explain the setting and introduce each character. For example, a situation might involve a kid at the house of a friend whose parents aren't home. The kid is being tempted to drink, perhaps with arguments like "My parents will never know." The skit might center on a conversation between the kid and his friend. After each skit, discuss other situations in which the temptation might occur.

SMALL GROUP

Step 2
"The Interview" skit on Repro Resource 4 probably wouldn't work well with a small group. Instead, have group members form teams of two or three. Distribute poster board and markers to each team. Assign each team one of the passages listed in the session. Instruct the teams to look up their assigned passage and then make a poster illustrating the concepts in the passage. For instance, the team that is assigned I Corinthians 10:1-13 might draw pictures of the Israelites being guided by a cloud, the bodies of the Israelites scattered across the desert, the Israelites bowing down to idols, the Israelites being killed by snakes, etc. Encourage the teams to convey the passages' ideas as thoroughly as possible in their posters. Give the teams a few minutes to work; then have each team display and explain its poster.

Step 4
In a small group, kids may feel more comfortable offering advice to others who are facing temptation. Distribute slips of paper and pencils. Instruct each group member to write down a temptation he or she is struggling with. Collect the slips and shuffle them, being careful to keep them anonymous. Then read the slips one at a time and have group members offer advice from Scripture, encouragement, and practical suggestions for handling the temptations.

LARGE GROUP

Step 1
A large group gives you a fairly decent sample for polling your group members. Distribute paper and pencils. Ask group members to answer the following questions anonymously, using only numbers. For each question, except the last one, they should write "1" for "never," "2" for "sometimes," and "3" for "often." The questions are as follows: **How often are you tempted to (1) use drugs or alcohol? (2) Cheat? (3) Steal? (4) Go too far sexually? (5) Swear? (6) Lie? (7) Destroy something? (8) Of these temptations, which is the toughest for you? Write the number of the question.** Collect and shuffle the papers, keeping them anonymous. Have several volunteers tally the results. They could list the questions in a column on the left-hand side of the board and write "Never," "Sometimes," and "Often" across the top. Then they could place a hash mark in the appropriate column for each response. While they are doing this, have the rest of the group discuss the attractions of each temptation and the possible negative results. When the tallies are finished, go over the survey. Use this information to guide later discussions to the areas that most tempt your group.

Step 2
With a large group and meeting area, you could stage an elaborate production of "The Interview" skit on Repro Resource 4. Choose a group member (or perhaps an adult leader) who is comfortable "hamming it up" in front of an audience to play the role of the interviewer. Make him up to look as much like Phil Donahue as possible. You might even record some of the *Donahue* theme music to play before the skit. Give the interviewer a microphone and other talk-show props. Encourage him to use a lot of Phil Donahue's mannerisms as he interviews various group members. You might even arrange the chairs in your meeting area to look like a talk-show audience set.

Step 1

Get your group members' attention by having them discuss why sin looks fun. Have them form teams. Instruct each team to come up with a list of the top ten reasons that sin is (or seems) fun. After a few minutes, have teams share their lists. If you like, combine the lists to make a top ten list for your whole group. Then discuss how these reasons make temptations so tempting. Ask whether the temptations (sins) are really all that they're cracked up to be. Help group members think about the possible negative consequences of giving in to some temptations.

Step 2

Motivate group members to study the passages carefully in order to prepare for a quiz game similar to the television show "Family Feud." Have group members form two teams. List the passages on the board. Instruct the teams to study the passages so that they can answer questions in the quiz. Have a "contestant" from each team stand in front of you facing his or her opponent. Put a chair or desk between the contestants. Use the questions on Repro Resource 4. When you ask a question, the first contestant to hit the chair gets to answer it. If the answer is correct, that person's team gets a point; if it's incorrect, the other contestant can answer. After the game, end the activity with the remarks in the session.

Step 2

Help your kids better understand a couple of the passages by providing them with some background information. For the I Corinthians passage, explain that Paul is using the history of the Israelites in the wilderness with Moses (following the cloud, crossing the Red Sea, eating manna) as an example of the dangers of giving in to temptation. At various times when the Israelites grumbled or rebelled, God punished them. For the Hebrews passage, explain that the writer is addressing Jewish Christians, comparing Jesus to the high priest in the Jewish religion. A high priest was someone who went before God as a representative of the people to ask God for forgiveness for the people's sins. Because Jesus died to save us from our sins and to restore our relationship with God, He is the "ultimate" High Priest. For the I John passage, explain that "atoning sacrifice" means that Jesus' death "paid" or made up for what we had done wrong.

Step 3

To help group members begin thinking about temptation, you might want to use a familiar representation usually found in the media (most notably in cartoons): angels and devils trying to influence a person's actions. Have group members form teams of three. Assign each team one of the temptations on Repro Resource 5. Explain that one team member will play Joe or Judy Junior High, one will play a devil, and one will play an angel. Give the teams a few minutes to prepare a skit in which the devil and angel try to get Joe/Judy to give in to or resist a temptation. Team members should begin the skit by explaining the situation (e.g., being tempted to drink). After the skit, have the rest of the group offer advice about how to avoid or overcome such a temptation.

Step 1

Get group members thinking about the process of temptation by having them draw flowcharts. Distribute pencils and paper. Have kids think about what happens when a person is tempted. What starts it? What makes the person resist or give in? How many opportunities does a person have to give in? When is it too late? Have group members diagram the process with boxes and lines. You might need to draw a sample flowchart on the board to give them the idea of what one looks like. Have group members share their charts and discuss any differences in their views of the process. Explain that today's session focuses on how to fight against temptation.

Step 5

Use Psalm 51 to guide your group in confessing situations in which they have given in to temptation, to admit to God the temptations that they struggle with, and to commit themselves to obedience with His help. Read verses 1-6 in unison. Then pause for a time of silent confession. Next, read verses 7-12 in unison. Then pause for a time for kids to admit to God the temptations they struggle with. Read verses 13-19. Then pause for a silent prayer of commitment to renewed obedience with God's help. Close with a sentence prayer, thanking God for helping us fight temptation.

Step 3

After "Create-a-Temptation" (Repro Resource 5) has been completed and discussed, ask your group members if some of the things on the sheet seem more appealing or tempting than others. Talk about the successes your group members have had in resisting these temptations. Ask: **How have you been able to avoid giving in to these temptations? What suggestions would you give to other kids who are facing these temptations?** Make a list of the suggestions on the board.

Step 4

After listing some fun things to do and discussing how to use God's help in resisting temptation, read together I Corinthians 10:1-13 and Hebrews 4:14-16. Have group members vote on which of these passages they, as a group, want to memorize. Then have group members form six teams. Assign each team one of the sections of the selected passage; have the team memorize its section so that team members can say it together in unison. After a few minutes, have each team recite its section in turn so that the entire passage is quoted by the group.

Step 1

Begin with a modified version of tug-of-war. You will need two milk crates (or sturdy boxes) and a six-foot piece of rope. Turn the crates over and place them about four feet apart. Have a guy squat on each crate and grab an end of the rope. The object is for each guy to pull his opponent off of his crate without getting pulled (or falling) off of his own. It can get tricky. If a player pulls very hard, his opponent may let his end of the rope go slack and upset the player's balance; so the players need to be savvy. (If you want more than two guys to play at once, you will need additional pairs of crates and ropes.) After everyone has played, have the guys compare the game to temptation. They might point out that with both it's a struggle to keep your balance, that you must be wary, and that it is easy to get fooled. Continue discussing temptation using the questions in the session.

Step 3

As you discuss the temptations on the sheet, help your group members focus on what aspect of the temptations are especially strong for junior high guys. For each temptation, ask: **What makes this activity especially attractive to guys? What makes it especially difficult to resist?** Encourage group members to discuss the pressure to be macho, tough, or cool.

Step 1

Play a game in which a person who is "It" tries to tempt the other players to smile. Have group members form a circle and choose someone to be "It." This person should approach someone in the circle and do whatever he or she can (within reason) to make that person smile. The person who is "It" may bribe, threaten, tell jokes, make funny faces, or do anything else— except touch the person—to make his or her victim smile. The victim, meanwhile, must keep repeating, "I see nothing to smile about." The person who is "It" has 30 seconds to make the victim smile. If the person doesn't smile in that time, the person who is "It" must choose another victim. If the victim does smile, he or she becomes "It." Afterward, have group members discuss how they resisted the temptation to smile. Then have them compare this temptation to others that they face.

Step 4

If possible, choose one of the clean fun ideas that group members came up with and use it to end the session. If you don't have any ideas that will work at the moment, play the following game—just for good, clean fun. Choose someone to be "It." This person's job is to guard his or her "treasure" (a handkerchief or some other easy-to-grab object, placed on the floor near the person's feet). He or she may not move from the spot where he or she is standing. The rest of the group members should circle around the person who is "It" and try to grab the treasure without getting touched. If the person who is "It" touches someone, that person must remain frozen in place until the game is over. If someone successfully grabs the treasure without being touched, he or she becomes "It." When a new person becomes "It," the people who were touched are "unfrozen." Play several rounds.

Step 1
Bring in as great a variety of media as possible (newspapers, magazines, songs, radio, television, etc.). Have group members search these media to find as many examples of temptations as they can. Encourage them to think about television shows, movies, and music videos that may not be represented in what you brought. Instruct group members to list or show examples of the temptations that they find. Some of temptations they might find include drinking alcohol, having sex outside of marriage, worshiping your own body, overindulging, and living selfishly. (Be careful that you don't offer temptations in your effort to study temptations. For example, you don't want to show scantily-clothed people to demonstrate things that tempt us to lust.) As group members share the examples they've found, have them discuss the attractions and dangers of these temptations.

Step 3
Have group members form teams. Give each team a tape recorder or a video camera. Instruct each team to make a public service message about fighting temptation. Assign each team one of the temptations on Repro Resource 5. Have the team consider why the action is tempting, reasons people give in, how to avoid the temptation, how the Bible could help, and how a Christian friend could help. The teams should develop messages that incorporate all of these ideas. For example, one team might stress that kids steal because they want an item, because they can't afford it, because they think nobody will miss it, or because their friends will think they're weird if they don't. Then the team might point out that the Bible condemns stealing. It might also remind kids that they could get in big trouble if they get caught stealing. Finally, the team might suggest that if a person is tempted to steal, he or she should go to the store only with Christian friends.

Step 2
You can condense this activity by eliminating the talk show component. Give the teams a few minutes to study their assigned passages. Then choose three or four questions (from Repro Resource 4) for each passage to ask the teams.

Step 3
Shorten this activity in the following manner: Have group members form six teams. Assign each team one of the temptations on Repro Resource 5. Instruct the teams to describe or draw a situation in which their temptation could occur. Then have each team share its temptation and situation. Briefly discuss other situations in which the temptation might occur; then use the questions in the session to discuss how to avoid or resist the temptation.

Step 2
To focus more specifically on urban temptations, use the following questions in your Bible study.
I Corinthians 10:1-13
• **What temptations are "common" to people in the city?**
• **God promises to "make a way to escape" temptations. How might He help someone escape the temptation of racism? Homosexuality? Sexism? Violence?**
Hebrews 4:14-16
• **If all of the Christians in this city were to approach God together in confidence to ask for one thing, what should they ask for?**
• **What are some of the hurts people have in your school that you think Jesus "sympathizes" with most?**
I John 1:5—2:2
• **What people in your community are sources of "light" for you to follow?**
• **How could the city be improved "if we confess our sins" to each other?**

Step 4
For a fun option, have a 1960's Motown-style production about temptation. Have group members form three teams. Inform the teams that they are the "Resist Temptations," and are about to be on TV. They must get a Christian message across to the world by harmonizing scriptural truth and performing a coordinated dance. Team 1 will address the issue of homosexuality in its production (Romans 1:18-32). Team 2 will address racism (Galatians 3:26-29). Team 3 will address drug abuse (I Corinthians 3:16, 17). Applaud all performances. Afterward, reflect on the importance of resisting temptation as a Christian.

Step 1
Ask for two or three high school volunteers to help you with the opening activity. These volunteers should try to persuade your junior highers to eat some of the treats you brought in. To make the situation more effective, you could leave the room and give your volunteers a chance to "work" without you around. Afterward, discuss how pressure from other people—especially people we like or people we want to like us—affects our response to temptation.

Step 4
Continue discussing ways of handling temptations by hosting a roundtable discussion. You will need three or four college-age volunteers to discuss honestly the temptations they faced in junior high and high school and the ways they handled those temptations. Before the discussion, give your group members a few minutes to come up with some questions. Suggest some of the following if they need help getting started: **What was one of the temptations you faced most often? How did you try to eliminate it? Knowing what you know now, if you had to go back to junior high or high school, what would you do differently?** Assure your volunteers that they can refuse to answer any questions they find too personal.

Step 2
Simplify the "interview" and Bible review by doing the first interview together as a group. Have volunteers take turns reading aloud I Corinthians 10:1-13. Then discuss it as a group and have group members respond to the interviewer's questions. Then have group members form two teams. Assign one team to look up and discuss Hebrews 4:14-16; assign the other team to look up and discuss I John 1:5–2:2. After a few minutes have the teams respond to the interviewer's questions.

Step 3
After your sixth graders have completed "Create-a-Temptation" (Repro Resource 5), have them talk about some of the temptations they face that aren't listed on the sheet. As a group, discuss ways to avoid and resist these temptations. Then ask: **Are some of the temptations on the sheet more tempting to kids your age than others? If so, which ones? Why do you think they're more tempting? Which of the temptations on the sheet are not tempting to you at all? Why do you suppose they're not tempting to you? What suggestions would you give to other kids who are tempted by these things?**

Date Used:

Approx.
Time

Step 1: Tempted! _____
o Extra Action
o Large Group
o Heard It All Before
o Fellowship & Worship
o Mostly Guys
o Extra Fun
o Media
o Combined Junior High/High School
Things needed:

Step 2: Book Review _____
o Small Group
o Large Group
o Heard It All Before
o Little Bible Background
o Short Meeting Time
o Urban
o Sixth Grade
Things needed:

Step 3: Personal Temptations _____
o Extra Action
o Little Bible Background
o Mostly Girls
o Mostly Guys
o Media
o Short Meeting Time
o Sixth Grade
Things needed:

Step 4: Good Clean Fun _____
o Small Group
o Fellowship & Worship
o Mostly Girls
o Extra Fun
o Urban
o Combined Junior High/High School
Things needed:

How to Be Christ's Body in the World

YOUR GOALS FOR THIS SESSION:

Choose one or more

☐ To help kids recognize that we as Christians are to be God's representatives in our world.

☐ To help kids understand what God wants us to do as His representatives.

☐ To help kids choose one thing they can begin doing to fulfill the tasks God has given us as Jesus' body.

☐ Other _____

Your Bible Base:

Mark 1:14-42
Romans 12:1-21
Galatians 5:22-25

Tic-Tac-Toe by Committee

(Needed: Chalkboard and chalk or newsprint and marker)

Have group members form two teams. Explain that each team will choose a representative to play a game of tic-tac-toe for the team. Draw a large tic-tac-toe game on the board. Then designate one team to start. Representatives must consult with their teams before every move; but once the representative steps to the board, teams must be silent until the representative places an X or O.

If group members enjoy the activity, play several games, with the teams taking turns going first. It's important, however, that teams keep the same representatives for each game.

Afterward, ask: **Who was playing tic-tac-toe here? Explain.** (Some group members may say that *everyone* was playing tic-tac-toe, and that the representatives were doing only what the teams told them to do. Others may say that only the two representatives were playing because, ultimately, the decisions about where to put the X's and O's were theirs.)

What is a representative? What is his or her job? (A representative is someone who acts on the behalf of others. Some people say the job of a representative is to do the will of the people he or she represents. Other people say the job of a representative is to *consider* the will of the people he or she represents, but then to act according to what he or she thinks is right.)

Where is the most obvious place we see representatives at work in our society? (Government.)

Have you ever been a representative for any group? Point out that two of your group members were representatives for their teams in tic-tac-toe. People who play on school sports teams or who compete in marching band contests could be considered representatives of their schools. If no one mentions it, point out that if a person is a Christian, he or she is automatically a representative.

STEP
2

The Androflopian Invasion

(Needed: Copies of Repro Resource 6, pencils)

Distribute copies of "The Androflopian Invasion" (Repro Resource 6) and pencils. Have group members work through the fictional situation on the sheet individually. You may want to read aloud the opening paragraph, to make sure everyone understands what to do.

Give group members about five minutes to complete the sheet. Then ask several volunteers to share what they came up with. After each volunteer shares, encourage the other group members to respond to his or her plan.

Use the following information to supplement group members' responses.

What exactly will you try to tell the people of Earth? (The message should be hopeful, yet subtle. The gist of the message should be that there is a way to solve the world's problems. Yet, you don't want to "scare people away" with your message.)

What will you do tomorrow to begin your task? (The first step probably would be to talk to people on a personal level, one-on-one. Get to know them, engage them in conversation, and gradually bring up the idea of hope for the future.)

What will you be doing in a month? (After a month, if you've got a group of people who are convinced that you're telling the truth, you might want to organize them and send them out to take the message to others.)

What will you be doing in a year? (After a year, depending on how many people are convinced of your message, you might want to begin a national campaign. This could include advertising, media exposure, mass-producing books to spread the message, etc.)

What will you be doing in four years? (Ideally, in four years, you'd like to have people taking the message overseas and to other countries. This would involve training those people on how to communicate with people of other cultures.)

Then ask: **As an Androflopian, were you a representative? If so, what did you represent? What was your assignment as a representative?** (As Androflopians, group members represented the people of Androflop. Their assignment was to tell the people of Earth about how the Androflopians could solve Earth's problems, and to prepare the way for the coming of the Androflopians.)

As Christians, who or what do we represent? What is our assignment as representatives? Your group members probably will know that we represent Christ. But they may not be entirely sure about what our assignment is. That's OK; don't force anyone to respond.

Explain: **We are God's representatives on the earth. We are His hands and His feet. We are His mouth. We are His body. And He wants us to function in a way that will prepare other people to meet Him. We're going to take a look today at what He expects of us.**

STEP

3

Job Descriptions

(Needed: Bibles, paper, pencils, chalkboard and chalk or newsprint and marker)

OPTIONS

LARGE GROUP

HEARD IT ALL BEFORE

LITTLE BIBLE BACKGROUND

MEDIA

SIXTH GRADE

Say: **If we're going to be God's representatives on earth, we need to know what kinds of things God wants done. To find that out, let's look at what Jesus did while He was on earth.**

Have group members form teams of three or four. Distribute paper and pencils. Instruct each team to read through Mark 1:14-42 and, based on the passage, come up with a job description for Jesus—a list of things Jesus did while He was on the earth. Each team should come up with a list of at least five things.

Give the teams a few minutes to work. When they're finished, have them share their lists with the rest of the group.

Some of Jesus' actions that teams might list include proclaiming the good news of God (vs. 14), calling disciples to follow Him (vss. 16-20), teaching with authority (vss. 21-23), casting out demons (vss. 23-26, 34, 39), healing the sick (vss. 30-34, 40-42), praying (vs. 35), and showing compassion for people (vss. 30-34, 40-42).

Afterward, ask: **Which of these actions do you think God wants us to do too? Why?** (We may not call disciples in the same way that Jesus did, but we can talk to people about following Him. We can teach others what we know of Jesus and His Word. We may not cast out demons or heal the sick, but we can pray for people who are suffering. And we certainly have the responsibility to show compassion for people as Jesus did.)

After a brief discussion, say: **God gave us more specific directions for what He wants us to do.**

Have group members reassemble into the teams of three or four they formed earlier. Instruct them to read through Romans 12 and, based on the passage, come up with a job description for Christians—a list of things we should be doing in the world. Each team should come up with a list of at least ten items. Teams may write their lists on the backs of the papers they used earlier.

Give the teams a few minutes to work. When they're finished, have them share their lists with the rest of the group. Write the teams' ideas on the board as they are named.

Some of the actions teams might list include giving ourselves to God (vs. 1), being different from the world (vs. 2), being humble (vs. 3), using our gifts (vss. 6-8), loving others (vs. 10), being joyful (vs. 12), praying (vs. 12), sharing with others (vs. 13), living in harmony with others (vs. 16), refraining from seeking revenge (vs. 19), feeding the hungry (vs. 20), and overcoming evil with good (vs. 21).

Ask: **Are there any other responsibilities for Christians that you can think of that weren't included in Romans 12?** If no one mentions it, suggest sharing our faith with others. Add any other suggestions group members come up with to the list on the board.

Refer to the list on the board, and ask: **How can we possibly hope to do all of these things?** Get a few responses. If no one mentions it, point out that no Christian can expect to fulfill all of these responsibilities alone. However, with God's help and with the help of other Christians, all of these responsibilities can be accomplished.

STEP
4

What Can We Do?

(Needed: Paper, pencils)

Point out that some of the items listed on the board could be done by your group as a whole. Have group members form teams of two or three. Distribute paper and pencils to each team. Instruct each team to choose an item on the board that could be done by your entire group—perhaps as a group project. For instance, "feeding the hungry" would be a great group project. Each team should then sketch out a plan for your group to follow in carrying out the chosen assignment. For example, plans for feeding the hungry might include holding a car wash

or some other fund-raiser, and sending the proceeds to a hunger relief organization. Another plan of action would be for your group to sponsor a child in a third-world country, through an organization like Save the Children.

As the teams are working, go around and help them with their ideas. Remind them of the limitations your group has, and encourage them to be creative within those limitations.

When teams are finished, have them report to the whole group to "sell" their idea. When all the teams have reported, have group members vote on which project to pursue. Ask for volunteers to head up the planning of the project.

Let your volunteer leaders help as you gather suggestions from the group on how to put your plans into action. Encourage group members to volunteer what they might be able to do. Remind them that they need to take seriously what they volunteer to do, because the rest of the group will be counting on them.

Getting Started

(Needed: Bibles, paper)

Say: **The group project we're planning is great. But there are some things on our list that we can do only as individuals. Let's put aside the group project and look back at the list.**

Have group members form pairs. Instruct each person to look over the actions on the list and choose one thing to work on in his or her life. Group members should then tell their partners what they've chosen and how they plan to work on it.

After a few minutes, say: **What we're planning to do as God's representatives is great. But remember, whatever we're doing for Jesus, we won't be doing it alone. The Holy Spirit is working in us to produce good fruit.**

Have someone read aloud Galatians 5:22-25. Then say: **If we're really seeking to live our lives for God and have made a faith commitment to Jesus Christ, the Spirit will always be there to help us. And with help from God's Holy Spirit, we can accomplish any mission He gives us!**

Close your session in prayer, asking God to help your group members as they seek to be Christ's body in the world.

The Androflopian Invasion

You're from the distant planet of Androflop, but your appearance has been altered so that you look like an average human. You've been sent here as a representative of the Androflopians. Your people plan to come to Earth eventually and help solve all the Earth's problems. Your mission is to convince the people of Earth to trust the Androflopians and look forward to their coming. The Androflopians will not come until your mission is accomplished. You have five years to complete your mission or you will be replaced. It's time to consider your strategy.

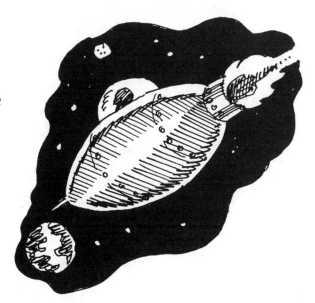

What exactly will you try to
tell the people of Earth?

What will you do tomorrow to begin your task?

What will you be doing in a month?

What will you be doing in a year?

What will you be doing in four years?

EXTRA ACTION

Step 1

For a more active variation of the opening game, you might have group members play "human tic-tac-toe." Rather than drawing the tic-tac-toe grid on the board, mark it out on the floor of your meeting area with masking tape. Make the grid as large as possible. (If your meeting area allows, each square should be at least six feet square.) The representatives will still consult with their teams about each move. However, rather than writing on the board, the representative will choose one of his team members and position that person accordingly on the floor. If the team has "X," the person chosen by the representative must lay on the floor with his or her arms outstretched in an "X" shape. If the team has "O," the person must curl up in an "O" shape. (Make sure representatives choose appropriately dressed people to serve as X's and O's.) Afterward, discuss the activity, using the questions in the session.

Step 2

Have group members form pairs. Have each pair brainstorm a list of different kinds of representatives. Then have the pairs choose one of the representatives on the list to act out while the rest of the group tries to guess what it is. If you think your group members will have trouble coming up with examples of representatives, you might make a list yourself, writing each example on a separate slip of paper. Then have each pair choose a slip and act it out. Your examples could include things like a door-to-door salesman, a politician, a policeman, thugs working for a crime boss, a writer's agent, a lawyer, etc. Afterward, discuss how the various representatives have tasks similar to the tasks of Christians.

SMALL GROUP

Step 1

Distribute paper and pencils. Explain to your group members that they will be selecting representatives from the group to do certain tasks. For each task, they should pick the person they feel is best suited for it. Here are some of the tasks you might use: giving a speech on behalf of the group, planning a ski trip for the group, setting up for a concert for the group, making a publicity poster for the group, writing the group's statement of purpose. (You might want to think of other categories, so that you have one for each person in the group. Group members would then have to assign a task to everyone.) When you're finished, have group members share their assignments and discuss why they felt the various people would be good representatives in those capacities.

Step 2

With a small group, you might want to have group members work on Repro Resource 6 together. A person working on the sheet individually might feel limited in predicting what he or she could accomplish alone. You'll need to alter the instructions on the sheet slightly. Have group members imagine that they're a *team* of representatives from Androflop. Together their job is to communicate the Androflopian message. Group members may decide to assign certain tasks to different pairs or teams. For instance, two or three of them may be in charge of infiltrating the media with their message. A couple of others may be responsible to carry the message to world leaders. A few others may be responsible for communicating the message to the "common people."

LARGE GROUP

Step 1

Have group members form teams of five for a five-part relay. You will need a large open space and five balls (soccer balls, volleyballs, or basketballs). Explain that the first player on the team will run across the room and back; the second player will hop across the room and back; the third player will bounce a ball while running across the room and back; the fourth player will dribble a ball soccer-style across the room and back; and the fifth player will crab walk across the room and back. The first team finished wins. Instruct the members of teams to find the best person for each "event." Afterward, point out that each player represented the team. Discuss the qualities of a good representative—knowing his or her job, doing it well, etc.

Step 3

Bring in samples of employment ads from a newspaper. Have group members form teams. Give one of the ads to each team. Have the teams study the ads and then read Romans 12. Then, based on that chapter, the teams will write employment ads for Christians (Christ's representatives). The ads should include descriptions of job duties, as well as necessary skills, experience, and attitudes. After a few minutes, have the teams read their ads. Then discuss the work of representing Christ.

Step 2

Have your group members try their hand at hostage negotiations. Explain that five people are being held hostage by terrorists and that a negotiator, representing the government, is trying to convince the terrorists to free them. Choose two or three group members to play the terrorists. Have them come up with a list of five demands, such as an airplane, a million dollars, or freedom for political prisoners. Choose two or three group members to play the government officials. Have them come up with a list of five guidelines for the negotiator, such as no safe passage to the airport, no money, and no freeing of political prisoners. Choose one person to play the negotiator. Equipped with the government's guidelines and the terrorist's demands, the negotiator should talk with the terrorists. The negotiator gets five tries to get the terrorists to accept a deal. Each time the terrorists refuse, a hostage is harmed. For the sake of the hostages, the negotiator must try to cut a deal as quickly as possible. If there's time, have group members switch roles and play again. Afterward, discuss the difficulties of being a representative in this situation. Have group members compare being a hostage negotiator with being a Christian.

Step 3

Kids who've been raised in the church may be especially attuned to spotting "hypocrisy" in Christians. Give them a chance to express their feelings. Distribute paper and pencils. After reading the Romans 12 passage, have group members draw a picture of an "ideal" Christian based on the passage. (For example, based on verse 20, they might draw a person carrying a bag of groceries.) Then have them draw a picture of "less-than-ideal" Christians in the same situation. (For instance, they might draw a person walking past a hungry-looking homeless guy on the street.) Afterward, discuss whether it's possible to be an "ideal" Christian and, if not, whether we should even try to be.

Step 3

Help your group members get a better grasp of the passage in Mark. Have them form teams of three or four. Provide each team with poster board and markers. Instruct the teams to read the passage and identify each separate task that Jesus performs in it. For each task, the teams should draw a cartoon depicting Jesus' actions. Team members could either divide up the tasks and drawings or work on all of them together. After a few minutes, have the teams share their cartoons. Discuss Jesus' activities, using the questions in the session.

Step 5

Your group members may have some difficulty coming up with practical ways to apply the actions they listed from Romans 12. Choose several of the general ideas you listed in Step 3, such as "being different from the world" or "living in harmony with others." Help group members brainstorm some specific ways of applying them to their lives. For example, they could "be different" by not swearing, not telling dirty jokes, by talking about God as if He really exists, by not lying to their parents, and so on. Cover as many of the items on the list as you can. Once you get them started, group members should have an easier time finding specific applications on their own. Have them choose one of these specific examples to work on and explain to a partner how they plan to do it.

Step 1

Use this idea to help kids learn more about each other and to introduce the idea of representatives. Have group members line up according to their birthdays, from the earliest in the year (January) to the latest. Then pair them off, the earliest with the latest, the next earliest and next latest, and so on. Give each person a pencil and a sheet of paper. On the top half of the paper, group members should write their partner's name; on the bottom half, they should write their own name. Without consulting with their partner, they should take the following quiz, giving the answers they think their partner would give. **(1) What's your favorite color? (2) What's your favorite food? (3) What's your favorite kind of music? (4) What's your favorite form of recreation? (5) What's your favorite school subject?** Next, have group members retake the quiz, answering for themselves. Then have them compare their answers. Instruct the partners to share how well they did, how well they knew each other. Afterward, discuss how good of a representative the various partners would make. (The better they know the partner, the better representative they would make.)

Step 5

Close the session with prayers of dedication for the group and individual projects. Your prayer time could follow the ACTS acrostic: Adoration, Confession, Thanksgiving, and Supplication. Have three teams write a sentence prayer, one for "adoration," one for "confession," and one for "thanksgiving." For "supplication," concentrate on the individual goals and group goal. To introduce individual goals, say: **We offer our bodies as living sacrifices.** Then give time for sentence prayers about the things individuals want to work on. To introduce the group goal, say: **We offer our group's service.** Again, give time for sentence prayers. Close after a few minutes.

Step 2

Have group members form three teams. Distribute copies of "The Androflopian Invasion" (Repro Resource 6) to each team. Instruct the teams to read through the sheet and then prepare a skit to demonstrate what they would do. Each team should choose one person to play the Androflopian and one person to play her assistant. The rest of the team members should play typical earthlings. Encourage the teams to make signs ("One Month Later," etc.) to indicate the passage of time in the skit. Give the teams a few minutes to prepare; then have them present their skits.

Step 5

As a group, identify the ideas listed on the board that an individual could do alone or with only two or three other people. Mark these ideas with an asterisk. Then have group members identify the ideas that could be done within the next week. Circle these items. Then instruct group members to choose from the ideas that are circled and have an asterisk by them one thing they plan to do in the coming week. Be sure to set aside some time in your next meeting to discuss how group members' projects went.

Step 1

Have your group members play a game in which teams compete by having their "champions" challenge one another. Divide into two teams and have each team choose a champion. Clear an area in your meeting room. Then give the champions one pillow apiece and let them have a 30-second pillow fight. The contestants score one point for every blow that lands cleanly on their opponent's torso. (You'll be the judge.). The contestants may not hit each other in the head. Members of the winner's team get to relax; members of the loser's team have to do five push-ups. Continue with another set of champions until all have participated. Afterward, discuss whether it was the individuals or the teams that won or lost the matches. Then talk about the advantages and disadvantages of being a representative.

Step 2

Divide into small groups. Have each group choose a favorite sports team. Instruct the members of each group to imagine that they are part of the publicity department for the team, responsible for developing a promotional plan. Have them consider how they will promote the team the next day, the next month, and the next year. How will they get more fans? What are their goals as a department? After each group explains its plan, have group members compare being publicity people to being Christians. (Both involve making a good impression, spreading a message, etc.)

Step 1

Play a group version of the "paper, rock, scissors" game. Have group members form two teams. For each round, the team will choose a representative to display the team's choice. Team members should confer about whether they want to show paper, rock, or scissors. When they've decided, the representatives from each team should face each other and, after a count of three, show their sign. (Remember: scissors cut paper, paper covers rock, and rock smashes scissors.) The losing representative must join the other team. If possible, play until one team loses all of its players. Then ask: **Who won or lost the individual rounds—the representative or the team?** Continue discussing the concept of representatives, using the questions in the session.

Step 5

One aspect of being a representative is following the example of your leader. In the following game, players will try to follow a leader so well that another player can't tell who the leader is. Send a volunteer out of the room. Have the rest of the group members sit in a circle. Choose someone to be the leader. The leader will clap, stomp, shrug, make faces, and so on. When he or she does so, the others should copy each motion. (You might want to play music so that group members can clap and stomp to the beat.) Bring the volunteer into the room and stand him or her in the middle of the circle. His or her goal is to guess which person is the leader. Give the volunteer three guesses. If he or she guesses correctly, choose someone else to leave the room; if not, send that person back out and appoint a new leader.

Step 1

You'll need several newspapers for this activity. Have group members form pairs. Distribute the newspapers among the pairs. Instruct the pairs to look through the newspapers to find as many examples of representatives as they can. Give them about five minutes to search. Then have the pairs share and explain the examples they found. From these examples, have your group members draw some conclusions about what a representative is and does. Then ask if any of your group members have ever been a representative.

Step 3

Play a recording of the Bruce Carroll song "Who Will Be Jesus" (from the album *The Great Exchange*). Then ask: **What do you think it means to "be Jesus" to someone else? What situations does the song describe in which someone could "be Jesus" to someone else? What are some other situations in which someone could "be Jesus" to another person? As representatives of Christ, what could we do in these situations?**

Step 2

If you're short on time, skip the activity on Repro Resource 6 entirely. After you finish with the tic-tac-toe tournament in Step 1, ask: **How many of you can name at least one member of the House of Representatives in Washington?** If your group is unusually astute, have a contest to see who can name the most representatives. Then ask: **Who or what do these men and women represent? What are their responsibilities as representatives?** Pick up Step 2 with the question **As Christians, who or what do we represent?** Then move into Step 3.

Step 4

To save some time here, simply have group members call out which of the items on the board could be done by your group. Have someone write down on a piece of paper the items that are identified. Rather than taking time to choose one of the items for your group to actually do and planning for the activity, save the list for another time. Move quickly to Step 5, in which group members identify items they could do individually.

Step 1

In your discussion of representatives, include the following question: **Do representatives always represent us the way we want?** The answer is no. In many cases, representatives are actually those who *aren't* acting in our best interests. Time after time those of the underclass have seen themselves pawned as the political refuse of misrepresentation and empty promises. Many urban teens believe they have no genuine representative. Ask: **Why is it that some representatives do such a bad job?** Bring the discussion around to the central issue: Some representatives fail to listen to those they are representing. Point out that this is similar to Christian representatives who fall hard. Perhaps they are sincere Christians, but they momentarily failed to represent God accurately. As a result, they were "impeached" as representatives. Help your Christian teens recognize that the only way they can adequately represent Jesus in this world is to *listen* to Him via prayer time, Bible study, and worship.

Step 5

To gain an understanding of how your teens believe their city can be changed for good during an "Androflopian invasion," replay the activity from Step 2 and localize the Androflop's assignment to your city or state. Explain that the Androflopian representatives have only three years to complete their assignment.

Step 2

After you've introduced the topic of representatives with the tic-tac-toe game and the "Androflopian invasion" activity, focus your discussion on a setting your group members can identify with: school. Ask group members to call out the qualities a person running for president of the student body should have. Point out that the president of the student body represents the students on the school board. If possible, you might want to keep track of junior highers' comments and high schoolers' comments in two separate columns on the board. After you've received several suggestions, ask your junior highers: **Do you think a high schooler would make a good representative for you on the school board? Why or why not?** (Probably not, because he or she may be too old to truly understand the wants and needs of junior highers.) Ask your high schoolers: **Do you think a junior higher would make a good representative for you on the school board? Why or why not?** (Probably not, because he or she doesn't have the "personal experience" needed to understand what high schoolers need and want.) Use this activity to lead into a discussion on what makes a good representative.

Step 4

Go through the actions you listed on the board, determining which ones would appeal more to junior highers (perhaps those that don't require transportation or those that don't involve a lot of personal responsibility) and which ones would appeal more to high schoolers (perhaps those that address a need that is currently in the news). As you decide on a group project, make sure you choose one that appeals to both age-groups.

Step 2

Distribute copies of "The Androflopian Invasion" (Repro Resource 6). Discuss as a group the mission of the Androflopian representative. Then have group members call out answers to the first question on the resource sheet. ("What exactly will you try to tell the people of earth?") Decide together on one answer for your group to use. Write this answer on the board. Then divide the group into four teams. Assign each team one of the remaining questions on the sheet. Instruct the team members to work together in planning a strategy. After a few minutes, have the teams share their strategies with the rest of the group.

Step 3

Rather than having group members form teams to explore Mark 1:14-42, do it as a group. Help your group members understand how to find the relevant facts in the passage. As group members call out the actions of Jesus described in the passage, write the actions on the board. After this list is finished and group members have an idea of how to search Scripture for specific information, have them form teams to work on Romans 12. The teams should look up the passage and make a list of the things Christians should be doing in the world. Give the teams a few minutes to work; then have them share their lists.

Date Used:

Approx.
Time

Step 1: Tic-Tac-Toe by Committee   _____
o Extra Action
o Small Group
o Large Group
o Fellowship & Worship
o Mostly Guys
o Extra Fun
o Media
o Urban
Things needed:

Step 2: The Androflopian Invasion   _____
o Extra Action
o Small Group
o Heard It All Before
o Mostly Girls
o Mostly Guys
o Short Meeting Time
o Combined Junior High/High School
o Sixth Grade
Things needed:

Step 3: Job Descriptions   _____
o Large Group
o Heard It All Before
o Little Bible Background
o Media
o Sixth Grade
Things needed:

Step 4: What Can We Do?_____
o Short Meeting Time
o Combined Junior High/High School
Things needed:

Step 5: Getting Started   _____
o Little Bible Background
o Fellowship & Worship
o Mostly Girls
o Extra Fun
o Urban
Things needed:

Custom Curriculum Critique

Please take a moment to fill out this evaluation form, rip it out, fold it, tape it, and send it back to us. This will help us continue to customize products for you. Thanks!

1. Overall, please give this *Custom Curriculum* course (*Basic Training*) a grade in terms of how well it worked for you. (A=excellent; B=above average; C=average; D=below average; F=failure) Circle one.

A   B   C   D   F

2. Now assign a grade to each part of this curriculum that you used.

a. Upfront article	A	B	C	D	F	Didn't use
b. Publicity/Clip art	A	B	C	D	F	Didn't use
c. Repro Resource Sheets	A	B	C	D	F	Didn't use
d. Session 1	A	B	C	D	F	Didn't use
e. Session 2	A	B	C	D	F	Didn't use
f. Session 3	A	B	C	D	F	Didn't use
g. Session 4	A	B	C	D	F	Didn't use
h. Session 5	A	B	C	D	F	Didn't use

3. How helpful were the options?
   - ❑ Very helpful
   - ❑ Somewhat helpful
   - ❑ Not too helpful
   - ❑ Not at all helpful

4. Rate the amount of options:
   - ❑ Too many
   - ❑ About the right amount
   - ❑ Too few

5. Tell us how often you used each type of option (4=Always; 3=Sometimes; 2=Seldom; 1=Never)

	4	3	2	1
Extra Action	❑	❑	❑	❑
Combined Jr. High/High School	❑	❑	❑	❑
Urban	❑	❑	❑	❑
Small Group	❑	❑	❑	❑
Large Group	❑	❑	❑	❑
Extra Fun	❑	❑	❑	❑
Heard It All Before	❑	❑	❑	❑
Little Bible Background	❑	❑	❑	❑
Short Meeting Time	❑	❑	❑	❑
Fellowship and Worship	❑	❑	❑	❑
Mostly Guys	❑	❑	❑	❑
Mostly Girls	❑	❑	❑	❑
Media	❑	❑	❑	❑
Extra Challenge (High School only)	❑	❑	❑	❑
Sixth Grade (Jr. High only)	❑	❑	❑	❑

6. What did you like best about this course?

7. What suggestions do you have for improving *Custom Curriculum*?

8. Other topics you'd like to see covered in this series:

9. Are you?
   ❑ Full time paid youthworker
   ❑ Part time paid youthworker
   ❑ Volunteer youthworker

10. When did you use *Custom Curriculum*?
    ❑ Sunday School   ❑ Small Group
    ❑ Youth Group   ❑ Retreat
    ❑ Other _____

11. What grades did you use it with? _____

12. How many kids used the curriculum in an average week? _____

13. What's the approximate attendance of your entire Sunday school program (Nursery through Adult)? _____

14. If you would like information on other *Custom Curriculum* courses, or other youth products from David C. Cook, please fill out the following:

Name: _____

Church Name: _____

Address: _____

_____

Phone: (____) _____

Thank you!